Reiki Masters Training Manual

A Means to Spiritual Awakening

Living Light Book Series 1

KAIA

Copyright 2014, KAIA

Reiki Masters Training Manual
A Means to Spiritual Awakening

Oji *(A Gift)* Publications, a Division of
Nuvo Development, Inc.
P. O. Box 373015
Decatur, GA 30037

ISBN 978-0-9719004-9-3

This Reiki Masters Training Manual is specifically dedicated to my three children, Kiara Afiya Bell, Fumiko Lee Aman and Nua KAIA Aman, the next generation of unfolding personal spiritual evolution, whom I love so dearly.

This book and others to come is part of your legacy for you to be proud of. It is an in-depth insight into your father so that you may know me for my essence and true life expression.

Secondarily, and certainly not least, this Reiki Training Manual is dedicated to all of the aspirants seeking spiritual unfoldment. May it aid you in your life's travels and propel you further into the depths of your divine and holy quest for the benefit of serving the beings of this planet.

Reiki Master's Training Manual
Healing Mantra of the Medicine Buddha

Hum,
Your body is the color of a mountain of Lapis Lazuli.
You dispel suffering of disease from all sentient beings.
Your retinue of the light of Bodhisattvas surround you.
I praise and pay homage to the
Buddha who holds the precious medicine.

In Sanskrit:

Namo bhagavate bhaisajya-guru-vaidurya prbha-rajaya
Tathagataya arhate samyak-sambuddhaya
Tadyatha Om,
Bhaisajye bhaisajye bhaisajya samudgate svaha!

In English:

May these sentient beings (list names)
Who are sick quickly be freed from sickness.
And may all of the sicknesses of these sentient
beings, mentally, physically, emotionally and
Spiritually never arise again, E ma ho...

In Chinese:

Na mo bo qie fa di
Bi sha she Ju
Lu bi liu li
Bo la po
He la she ye
Da tuo jie duo ye
E La he di
San miao san pu tuo ye
Da zhi tuo nan
Bi sha shi, Bi sha shi, Bi sha she
San mo jie di Suo he.

Acknowledgements

Thanks, honor and respect to my mentors and the lineage masters for assisting me on the path of growth towards the illumination of my spirit.

Thanks to **Jean Lawrence and Zoe Yonnatis;** may peace and blessings fill their lives and may joy and happiness fill their spirits.

Reflections of a Master Initiation

*As resistance fades,
The melancholy drifts from my heart.
Vision clear -
Letting go of illusions hurts no more.
Grief loosens -
I can set the past free
As I rise to my birthright.
I set foot into the illumination that has been waiting,
Eagerly awaiting...
This peace is ineffable!*

*My spirit rejoices! Graceful images of dance, pass through my mind,
Organizing into unity my gifts.
Love has been conveyed;
Truth revealed. Grace rises, healing infinity...*

*Thank you, mighty companion, Kiel,
Graciously,* **Erin Leigh Bowman**

KAIA and Russell Holcombe a lineage successor

Reiki Lineage

Dr. Usui
Dr. Chujiro Hayashi
Hawayo Takato
Barbara Ray
Virginia Sandahl
Iris Ishikuro
Arthur Robinson
Jean Lawrence
Robin Scott Manna – Kiel Akma Iel Aman

Yuli Qian *(Lineage Successor under Kiel Aman)*

Russell Holcombe *(Lineage Successor under Kiel Aman)*

KAIA Reiki Brazilian Representative:
Andréa Carla Ribeiro da Silva)

大光明兵神

(Da Guang Ming Bing Shen)
"The Great, Bright White Light Protector"

New Usui Reiki Attunement

To receive you're New Usui Reiki Attunements, Level 1,2,3:

Sit in a comfortable relaxed position with the palms of your hands facing up, recite the words below and remain in this posture for 15-20 minutes to receive the energy. Use this process for receiving all of the attunements contained within this book.

"I now accept my New Usui Reiki Level 1,2 and 3 attunements created for me by Kiel Aman."

The Attunements will then, as default, transmit and begin to saturate your body with its energies.

You should sit with the energy for about 24hrs before using it to assimilate the new energy.

Preliminary Understanding for the Use of Reiki Healing Energy

1. When starting a healing treatment say "Reiki Flow. This will allow the Reiki energy to transmit for healing.

2. When completing a treatment say "Reiki Abide." This will discontinue the flow of healing energy and allow it to remain and circulate within the body environment of the client.

3. Say "I cut all strands" - three times to disconnect the link that was created between you and your client.

KAIA Reiki

The Efficient Synthesis of the Ultraviolet Ray of Light

Violet Color Ray

Vajra: Durable luminous light
KAIA: Universal guide
Reiki: Spiritual energy

"The Durable Luminous Light Ray of Universally Guided Spiritual Energy"

Table of Contents

	Page
Introduction	1
Reiki and Raku Kei	2
How to Channel the Reiki Energy	2
Healing Sessions	2
Reiki: What is it and How Does it Work?	3
Section 1	7
About Reiki	7
Laws of Vibration	8
Emptiness Relaxation Meditation	10
Spirit Guide Meditation	15
The Seven Glandular Healing Breaths	15
Black Light vs. White Light	24
Glandular Correspondences	25
Keys to Channeling Reiki	25
Self-Healing Circuit	27
Cho Ku Rei (Power Symbol)	28
Healing With the Cho Ku Rei	30
Triangle of Life Force	34
Section 2	35
Five Principles of Reiki	35
Reiki Science	37
Healing with Reiki Energy	38
Se He Ki	44
Working With the Sei He Ki	46
Section 3	51
Healing Hands Invocation	51
Chakra Meditation 7:1 Root 1:7	51
Raku Rei	54

	Page
Section 4	61
Kanji	63
Standard Reiki Healing Sequence	63
Section 5	67
Hon Sha Zah Sho Nen	67
Working with the Hon Sha Zah Sho Nen	72
Section 6	75
Dai Koo Myo Master Symbol	75
Igniting the Body of Light	80
Prayer Formula	90
The Laws of U	91
Sensitivity and Pain	92
Expressions of Reflections	93

INTRODUCTION

Reiki and RakuKei

'Reiki' originates from the words RAKU and KEI. Raku (Anale) is the vertical energy flow of spiritual fire, while (Vishudhe) is the horizontal flow of the spiritual fire of self improvement based upon origins that go back to ancient Tibet. In the beginning, Reiki calligraphs were painted upon large wall hangings and were used as the center of focus within Mantric workings (recitation of mantra's) for the enlightenment of Tibetan Holy Men in the monasteries. The participants would sit upon four-legged wooden stools in the center of an earthenware container, oval in shape to represent the akasa (etheric egg). The container was filled with three inches of water, and the stool sat in its center. The stool was composed of wood with a pure silver inlay in a channel up each of the four legs, which, in turn, connected to a cubical silver inlay upon the seat. One wall of the Tibetan temple was composed of copper, polished to the highest sheen imaginable. To the rear of the aspirant was an angled wall containing the Lama's prayer and the calligraphs of the Reiki symbols. The symbols were reflected by the copper wall and meditated upon by the participating initiate as he sat upon the stool in the center of the vessel filled with water. The idea was that one could implant the symbols deep into the subconscious mind through concentration, thus raising the consciousness and heightening one's awareness, while a purification of the body/mind continuum occurred. As this practice of Raku Kei was an esoteric science passed on by word-of-mouth, it eventually disappeared. Then, in the mid-1800s, Dr. Mikao Usui rediscovered in an ancient Sanskrit text, the symbols used as the catalyst for the meditation technique.

In the beginning, the Reiki calligraphs were only used for self-development in meditation and spiritual purification. Then, Dr. Usui made his discovery, causing the system to undergo many changes. Although the calligraphs remain basically the same, a revision has been made in order to allow the calligraphs to appeal to the Western mind by the simplicity of its rendering. The true system takes many days of intense concentration and memorization, coupled with exercise and seated hand and body postures.

Reiki is intended to be used for personal development and to gain a high self-awareness exercise in the expansion of human consciousness.

How to Channel Reiki Energy

Reiki is a healing energy that is transmitted through your hands, the hands of the channel who has been 'attuned'. REIKI energy comes from the Creator and you are simply the conduit, allowing the 'light' to pass though you into the receptor (whatever your hands touch). Once you are attuned to Reiki energy, it always flows; as once the light has been turned on, it cannot be turned off.

The channel is a healing instrument for only the highest and best of light. A person who receives Reiki is simply made better by becoming more closely in tune with their nature. One does not have to be sick or in a negative aspect of mind in order to benefit from Reiki channeling.

Healing Sessions

A Reiki healing session usually takes a minimum of an hour. It has been my experience that the person coming to the channel for healing will determine the time-frame.

Remember that as you channel the Reiki energy, you, as the channel, are also receiving healing on some level, whether on the physical, mental, emotional or spiritual level. Reiki is a soul and universal life energy that works on all four (mental, physical, emotional and physical) levels in the attuned person. Your energy level will become stronger as you channel the energy. Since the energy is technically never turned off, your energy will constantly build. On a soul and spiritual level, it has been my experience that Reiki energy works internally, creating many changes that start on the etheric level and then manifest at the physical level.

It is believed that we have been incarnated at this time in the world's evolution to heal ourselves and others. Every encounter is a "Holy Instant." As such you should honor and respect who and what you are as a "Light Being," for as you honor and respect yourself, we honor and respect others. As we honor and respect others, we honor and respect ourselves. Allow your LIGHT TO SHINE.

Reiki: What is it and How Does it Work?

Reiki is part of the life force of the universe. It is the magnetism of the spirit integrating into the form of man. Reiki is the force of what we call light: the light of the love of the universe. Reiki is what we all are a part of (one light, one life, one heart) and is the spiritual force used to unite ourselves to our true identities as spirits.

Reiki is a life force energy that is gathered and accumulated from the universe. After receiving Reiki attunements, you can channel this energy through your body into the bodies of others to facilitate healing. Reiki is a passive (feminine) energy that allows the body to heal in a comfortable and subtle manner.

Reiki energy is channeled using Reiki symbols, which create an energy matrix that magnetizes to your body and then radiates from it. This energy is attracted of the channel in the form of white light known as photons.

This white light energy penetrates every cell in the body and subtly increases the electro-magnetic energy field, filling the body with light (Qi). This energy can be used to heal oneself or others.

The energy from the symbols radiate from within and focuses intrinsically, utilizing etheric matrix force fields. With this symbol energy reference in mind, Reiki attunements raise the vibrations of our minds and spirits. These Heightened energy vibrations are passed through the hands and eyes. Reiki energy applies higher level light energies to the denser energy fields within the afflictions within our bodies. This higher level of light allows this light to purify and heal damaged cells and tissues.

This *Reiki Master's Training Manual* is an instruction manual on how to focus, attract and utilize this energy source in a practical and simplistic manner. Numerous short treatment methods exist that are easy-to-learn and can be applied to yourself as well as to others. Reiki energy works through pacifying your nervous system, relaxing the tissues of your body and then energizing your cells. Thus, Reiki energy is useful in healing all types of stress-related disorders and pain. This book contains methods that can be used to, for example, energize and cleanse the endocrine glands and treat adrenal exhaustion, stress disorders and mental anxiety.

In order to utilize Reiki energy, we must understand four forms of spirit. The first form is the spirit of the higher self, which is what we call the inner spirit of the true self or the guiding spirit. Second is the spirit of the ascended self or what we call our master teacher of the higher self. Third is the spirit of the soul or the historical self.

Fourth is the spirit of oneness, which is the spirit of the family grouping of which each of us is cosmically a part. This form is the force of identity that Reiki clears the path toward personal enlightenment of the soul.

There are three levels to Reiki: **Association, Illumination and Integration**

The first level, Association, raises the consciousness of your own personal character and what you consider to be your shortcomings. This level presents you with a mirror that shows you what you have done to cope and survive in your life.

The second level, Illumination, allows you to see how you have created unnecessary patterns in your everyday life. This level presents you with the understanding of what needs to be accomplished in regard to changing the unnecessary patterns that you have created. This level can be a critical stage in the development of your spiritual growth. This level can also involve much turmoil due to self-evaluation that can usually be the motivating factor for great spiritual unrest.

The third level, Integration, helps you to gather all unharmonious conditions and bring them into balance. This level can open the way for great spiritual healing by allowing for the integration and harmonization of the emotional pain of facing up to your true inner self and opens the way to the four paths that lead to the oneness of spirit.

Reiki heals the four dimensions of the body-mind (physical, mental, emotional and spirit) and integrates the primary essence of the universe (the vibration of love) into the four dimensions of the body. The love vibration is the greatest force of spirit and is the binding force of life.

A Means to Awakening Spiritual Light

KAIA and Yuli Qian a lineage successor

SECTION 1

About Reiki

- **Rei** means light and **ki** means life force. Reiki is the knowledge and wisdom used to understand the energy patterns of life.

- Reiki attunements heal the Heart Chakra.

- Reiki allows the person being attuned to channel and receive life force energy. It is one of the few modalities that allows one to heal him or herself.

- The Reiki energy vibrates unconditional love and is activated through the Heart Chakra.

- The choice must be made by the recipient to let go of resistance and receive the Reiki energy openly and freely in order to manifest the best results.

- Reiki allows one the opportunity to release emotional pain (negative experiences in life).

- Due to Reiki's yin (receptive) nature, Reiki energy has a will of its own and knows where to go.

- Reiki energy grounds down from the universe to the Earth.

- Reiki is a female nurturing energy and is attuned to the feminine side of one's nature.

- Reiki is a light energy and attracts to the channel by way of photons. Physical energy loss is caused by over validation through self doubt.

- Reiki symbols emit minute piezo-electrical energies. Second degree symbols have a more powerful effect upon the body / mind / spirit continuum than does the level one attunement. The third degree symbol has a unique quality of its own that allows for the permanent locking in of energy to a person, place or thing; plus the visual impact of the practitioner's mental prowess and concentration ability in the formation of the mental imagery of the master symbol. The symbols work because of the attunements we receive; The symbols are embedded into the subjective mind and within the crown chakra. The symbols will not work properly without the Reiki Channel first completing the attunement process.

Laws of Vibration

Vibration is the acceleration of the frequency of the body where the spirit (the light of the soul) resides. The vibratory rate of a person is dictated by his ability to channel light.

The Five Standard Vibrations

Vibration 1: Physical Plane
Vibration 2: Mental Plane
Vibration 3: Spiritual Plane
Vibration 4: Soul Plane
Vibration 5: Universal Plane

The first vibration reflects the physical plane of existence. It is associated with the physical reality of the material world and is related to the environment as our physical body interprets it. We associate ourselves with our immediate surroundings and relate these surroundings to our inner bodies.

The second vibration reflects the mental plane of existence. It involves how the mind interprets its surrounding environment and relates to our ability to use discernment in what we believe and what we think. The mental plane is the means through which we validate our existence to ourselves and is the natural way by which we work our way through our everyday lives.

The third plane reflects the spiritual plane of existence. This plane is the heart of life and where we are allowed to relate our conscious thoughts to our physical reality. This spiritual vibration is one of great importance to our growth and development in regard to feeling our connection to the source of our existence. We are, by nature, spiritual bodies, but our physical and mental capacities can stifle the evolutionary progress towards ascension. We need to become open spirits with pure intentions in order to reflect this vibration.

The fourth vibration reflects the soul plane of existence and is where we manifest our reality into the essence of our creation. We are able to feel the life force through our entire being. We are a reflection of why we were created. This level helps us to understand why we are under the soul levels that we are under and how to ascend to the next level of our journey.

The fifth vibration reflects the universal plane of existence. This level is the vibration of oneness with the force of universal light, where the soul meets the creator and unconditional love manifests itself into the universe. This vibration is the level to which we all aspire in our journey from the corporeal essence to the universal essence. Our divine spirit created us to create this level.

Emptiness Relaxation Meditation

Recitation: Pause approximately four to six seconds between each sentence

Part I
Get comfortable
Become completely relaxed
Close your eyes
Take a deep breath
Hold the breath
Let your breath out slowly and completely
Concentrate your attention behind your eyes
Relax all of the muscles in your eyes
Relax the muscles in your eyes completely
Relax your eyes so much that they won't open
Relax them
Test your eyes to make sure that they are relaxed
If they are relaxed, they won't open
Now, take another deep breath
Hold it
Exhale slowly
Let your relaxation go all the way to your toes
Let go completely
Using your imagination
Prepare yourself to go beyond yourself
From this point on, let all outside noises
Increase your attention on my voice
Relax your toes completely
Concentrate all of your attention on your feet
Just let go
Relax all of the muscles in your legs
Concentrate on relaxing them now
First, relax your lower legs
Now, relax your upper legs

Concentrate on relaxing your hips
Relax your lower abdomen
And your stomach
Relax your lower back
Relax your chest
And your upper back
You are still aware of what is going on around you
You are able to hear me clearly
Relax the muscles in your shoulders and neck
Relax your arms all the way down to your fingertips
Now concentrate on relaxing your jaw
Just let it hang
Relax your tongue
Now relax all of the muscles in your face
Your mouth
Your eyes
Your chin
And your forehead
You are very deeply relaxed now, but not out of touch with reality
You are very much in tune with everything I say
You are completely aware of your surroundings
You are just very, very deeply relaxed

Part II
You have reached a level of deep physical relaxation
Let's concentrate on deep mental relaxation
I will count slowly down from 100 to 98
Double your relaxation with each number
When I reach 98, just let the number vanish
Here we go
100
Now double your relaxation
Just let go
99
Double again your relaxation
98

Double your relaxation one more time
Let the numbers vanish
This stage is a nice stage of relaxation
You are not out of touch with reality
You are deeply in tune with everything I am saying
You are completely aware of your surroundings
You are very intent upon my voice

Mentally repeat the following affirmation:
'In the province of the mind there are no limitations'
'In the province of the mind there are no limitations'
'In the province of the mind there are no limitations'
'In the province of the mind there are no limitations'
'In the province of the mind there are no limitations'
'In the province of the mind there are no limitations'
'In the province of the mind there are no limitations'
'In the province of the mind there are no limitations'

The next time you go into meditation, you will go even deeper
It will work better and faster and put you into a deeper state
Now you will move to the higher side of yourself
Pure spirit
A being of light
You are not your body
Concentrate your attention on your toes
Notice that you have toes
And that they are relaxed
But you are not your toes
Notice your feet now
And your lower legs
And your upper legs
You are not your legs either
As you relax even more, continue to concentrate your attention on my voice
Notice that you have hips,
But you are not your hips

Notice your stomach
Your chest
Your breathing going in ... and out
You are not your stomach
You are not your chest
And you are not your breathing
Notice your entire back
That is not who you are either
Notice your shoulders
You are aware that they are there
They are yours
But you are not your shoulders
And you are not your arms either
Notice that you have a neck
But you are not your neck
Switch your consciousness to your jaw now
You are not your jaw
And you are not your tongue
You are not any of the muscles in your face
Including your nose
Your eyes
And your mouth
You are not those
Notice your thoughts
You are not your thoughts
Go even deeper now
Give me your full attention
Concentrate completely on my voice
It is now time to raise your vibration with feelings of
 unconditional love
And strong positive thoughts
Surround yourself with a beautiful canopy of protective, white light
This white light represents truth and forgiveness and
Your ideal concept of the source of all that is good
Picture this white light starting to glow in your heart now
Allow this white light to glow in your heart

Allow it to increase
Feel its warmth
Feel its purity
Allow this feeling to extend
And radiate out of your heart
Until it completely envelopes your entire body
Allow it to completely surrounding you in a cocoon of pure, vibrant, white light
This white light is the source's perfect presence
You may actually see it, feel it or sense it,
But all you really need to do is to know it is there
It will always be with you
You now have the protection
Of this canopy of pure white light all around you
So that your subconscious mind is only open to suggestions
Helpful and beneficial to you
Bathe yourself in this white light
Notice that you are this white light
You are pure spirit
A dearly beloved child of the source
Beyond time
Beyond space
Feel this white light extending
Emanate your light into infinity
You are pure light
Unconditional, pure love
Pure compassion
Pure forgiveness
As you are now beyond the beyond
You are one with the universal
The ultra clear light of all bliss
The emptiness of all phenomena

Spirit Guide Meditation

Sit quietly in a comfortable position.
Focus your attention on your third eye center.
Take your mind to the center of the inside of your mind.
See a doorway full of light in your mind and walk toward it.
Walk through the arched doorway to the center of a round room filled with locked doors. Turn around clockwise until a particular door catches your attention.
Face the door and walk toward it.
Reach into your right pocket and pull out a key to unlock the door.
Enter the room and meet your spirit guide.
Give a gift to your spirit guide and wait until your guide gives you a gift in return.

Leave the room when you are ready.
Lock the door behind you.
Mark the door with a symbol that you will recognize.
Go back to the center of the room.
Turn counter clockwise to find the open archway.
Leave through the arched doorway and into the darkness into the center of your mind.
Come forward the center of your third eye.
Open your eyes.

The Seven Glandular Healing Breaths

The seven glandular breaths are necessary to elevate the primary essences of the physical body. They assist in accepting the higher vibrations of the spiritual body, which occurs when the etheric web is strengthened, allowing the spirit to utilize the web matrix to place its energies into the physical environment without overloading the nervous system.

This stepping down process is accomplished through abiding by the yin and yang matrix formula of uniting fire with water.

Fire is related to the breath of air, which, if over stimulated, can dehydrate the blood, overheat the tissues and burn out the nerve endings. Water is related to the blood circulation, which carries nutrients to the entire cellular body, and, if over stimulated, leads to a flooding of the channels and the creation of stagnation, which leads to the suffocating the vital life force.

When one undertakes the seven glandular breaths, one must first drink a glass of water to create a steam through which the elixir of the spiritual force must work its way. When finished with the exercises, one must lubricate the nostrils with ghee (clarified butter) to hydrate the mucous membranes and nourish the brain, keeping it from overheating. Once every four days, one should eat ½ a teaspoon of ghee along with ¼ a teaspoon of honey in order to protect the oja's (vital lubricating essence). This ghee and honey supplement will assist in harmonizing the fire and water of the body environment.

Yin and yang also reflect the outer environment, being the expression of our manifest qualities (masculine), and the inner environment, being the hidden principle of the potential qualities yet untapped (feminine). These two qualities must be harmonized in order to allow for the full expression of the higher spirit into its lower form.

Fire and water circulate throughout our body environment and fire animates the life force to motivate the water to flow. Water circulates the motivated life force by carrying and distributing it throughout the body. Each element is independent, yet interdependent upon the other.

Love is magnetic attraction.
Love is the binding force of life.
Love allows for all things to work together in cooperation.

Electric energy is the energy of spirituality.
Magnetic energy is the energy of material form.

The electrical force is conducted through the nervous system.
The magnetic force is conducted through the seven tissues.

The seven tissues are plasma, blood, muscle, fat, bone/marrow, nerves and sexual fluids.

Electro-magnetic energy is the union of spiritual forces into a physical reality.

If you are focusing on spiritual work, you must be sure to take in adequate fluids (water).

Water is essential for conducting the electrical force in order to protect the material body from burning out.

The combined force of water and nervous impulses is essential for recharging the adrenal body (the magnetic cohesive element).

An overstimulated adrenal body needs to utilize distilled water to remove the excess overcharged positive ions.

An underactive body environment needs to utilize mineral water to activate and bind the negative ions.

Therefore, it is essential to drink plenty of water and know which type is needed.

Kidney Breath (Earth Element)
Chakra 1: Adrenal Glands
Day: Tuesday

This breathing method is used to revive the life force by strengthening the kidney/adrenals. It is used to transmit the life force from one to another known and is known as the breath of initiation.

Assume a comfortable seated position and then inhale into the kidney region, expanding the lower back and visualizing the color of deep blue. Exhale through the nose.

You have completed one cycle.
Repeat these actions for 9-18-27 cycles.

3.3.6.3. Breath (Water Element)
Chakra 2: Sexual Glands
Day: Saturday

This breathing method is used to develop the Qi (life force) and prepare the body to receive and assimilate energy. It is the breath of the emotions and the breath that washes away despair. It takes you to the mirror of your soul and gives you access to enter the veil of darkness that you have created for yourself. It assists in healing the disturbances of the genitalia and is used to bring peace of mind.

When you inhale expand the abdomen and when you exhale while retracting the abdomen. Each breath is done with the mouth closed.

Assume a comfortable seated position. Inhale for the count of three, hold the breath and contract the anal sphincter for the count of three. Exhale for the count of six, while releasing the contraction. Hold the exhaled breath and contract the anal sphincter for the count of three.

You just completed one cycle. Repeat for 9-18-27 cycles.

Bated Breath (Fire Element)
Chakra 3: Pancreas
Day: Thursday

This breathing method is used to ignite the digestive fire and invigorate the digestive system. This breath is the flame of spirit and is used to prepare the body to receive energy work and purification. It burns away obstructions toward ascension by raising dormant or repressed emotions.

Assume a kneeling position on a floor mat positioned between your feet. Rest your hands on your lap. Inhale deeply through your nose. Exhale with a short, but continuous breath using the sound of Sa, Sa, Sa. Upon each short exhale, gently contract the pit of your stomach. Inhale and then slowly and gently tighten every muscle in your body, while holding your breath for the count of seven. Then, release the tension completely with a sudden exhale, while making the sound "AH." Repeat the cycle in a series of seven sets.

Heart Permeating Breath (Air Element)
Chakra 4: Thymus
Day: Wednesday

This breathing method is used to generate a field of radiation that expands the healing power of the auric field and connects the physical heart with the spiritual heart (thymus gland), activating the heart of the Buddha.

Assume a comfortable seated position with your eyes closed. Inhale into the heart center from three directions at the same time: from the perineum to the heart center, from the crown to the heart center and from the upper back to the heart center. Hold your breath for the count of seven, while tightening the huiyin point (anal contraction). Exhale through the front of the heart center, allowing for the breath to naturally dissolve into emptiness.

You just completed one cycle. Repeat for 9-18-27 cycles.

The Heart Permeating Breath has 4 paths:

- **Heart Consolidation**: Using the Heart Permeating Breath, circulate the field of radiation within the self with your hands placed over your heart center, the left hand under the right.

- **Heart Radiation**: Using the Heart Permeating Breath, radiate the field of healing to a distant loci with your hands placed palms outward and held in front of the heart. Using your mind recite the passage below.

May the love of the one soul radiate upon you, (person's name),
And permeate every part of your body;
Healing, soothing, strengthening and dissipating
All that hinders service and good health, Reiki Flow, Reiki Heal.

- **Heart Release**: Using the Heart Permeating Breath the client needing release sits perpendicularly in front of you in lotus. Place your left hand in front of your client's heart center and your right hand at the back of your client's heart center. Using your mind recite the passage below.

Blessed are those who are meek at heart.
Blessed are those who release the fears of despair.
Blessed are those who accept the goodness of life.
For these are of those whose hearts shall inherit the Earth.

*You are now ready to accept the heart of your soul,
so we are ready to shower your being with the light of love.
You are now within the company of your illuminated spirit,
Reiki Abide.*

- **Heart Union**: Instruction should be provided at the discretion of the teacher.

Breath of Consciousness (Ether Element)
Chakra 5: Thyroid
Day: Monday

This breathing method awakens and cleanses the entire cellular system, oxygenating and detoxifying the entire chemistry of the body. It allows the spiritual force of light to enter the body environment and is known as the rebirthing breath used to access the higher self.

Assume a comfortable seated or supine position. Open your mouth widely without using too much tension. Inhale by first expanding your abdominal cavity and then your chest cavity within one sequence. Exhale quicker than the inhale by letting the breath naturally fall out. Immediately following the exhale, repeat the inhaling sequence. Remain as relaxed as possible throughout the entire sequence.

Repeat for 27-54-108 breaths.

Alternate Nostril Breath (Ether Element)
Chakra 6: Pituitary
Day: Friday

This breathing method balances the Ida and Pingala channels (fire and water channels).

Due to the pituitary gland being the master gland of the body, this pranayam (breathing method) heals the entire body through the endocrine system. When one can breath equally and freely through both nostrils, one can say the channels in the entire body are clear and one is in optimum health.

Assume a comfortable seated position. Make a fist with your left hand thumb at the root of your pinkie finger and then place your left fist, turned up, next to your right ribcage at your elbow level. Your right fist will have the same hand formation, but with your index finger extended. Place the back of your index finger against the outside of your left nostril sealing the air passageway and inhale through your right nostril. Imagine a great, white light entering your nostril and filling your heart. Exhale through your right nostril and imagine all of the negativity that you have accumulated leaving your body in the form of black smoke. Move your index finger from your left nostril to your right nostril. Repeat the process that you just completed for your left nostril. Place your right palm into your left palm at your navel level. This time, inhale and exhale through both nostrils using the above process.

You have completed one cycle. Repeat for 9-18-27 cycles.

Hong Sau Meditation

The Hong Sau Meditation can be utilized to take you into a deep sense of relaxation simply by inhaling through the third eye center all the way down to the root of your spine, *while mentally chanting "Hong"* and then exhaling through the third eye returning from your spine, while mentally chanting "Sau."

Buzzing Breath: This breathing method is used to calm the mind and dissipate the accumulation of stress. Inhale and exhale through the posterior nasal cavity invoking a continuous and audible humming sound. Repeat for at least 30 seconds, but no more than a minute.

Elementary Brain Adjustment (Ether)
Chakra 7: Pineal
Day: Sunday

The following elementary adjustment will change the third layer of the neurons in a single rhythm and regulate the first ring under the stem of the brain. This breathing method will cause the back area of your head to vibrate. It will send oxygen directly to your brain, stimulating your pituitary gland and fixing the vibrator, which is called the pineal gland.

Assume a comfortable seated position. Use your thumb to touch the base under your Earth (baby) finger. Your Earth (baby) and water (ring) fingers must fold down on top of your thumb, holding it in place. Your fire (middle) and air (index) fingers should remain straight. Bend your elbows, keeping your forearms parallel to the ground. Your hands should be held level with the heart center with your palms facing downward and your fire (middle) and air (index) fingers pointing toward each other in front of the heart center.

Make an "O" shape with your mouth, while inhaling through your rounded mouth and exhaling forcefully through your nose. The force of the exhale will cause your nose to wrinkle up.

As you exhale through your nose, your hands and forearms should move outward so that your fire (middle) and air (index) fingers point straight out away from you. When you inhale through your mouth, return your arms to their original position. Throughout this breathing method, focus your attention on the tip of your nose.

Perform seven breaths to complete one cycle. Repeat for 9-18-27 cycles.

Upon completion of this breathing method, inhale deeply and hold your breath for ten seconds, while locking your back molars and gently tightening every muscle in your body. Exhale forcefully while saying "breath of a cannon" through your mouth. Repeat twice more.

Black Light vs. White Light

- **Black Light**: <u>absorption,</u> accumulation, creation, mystery

    o Black is the fullness of color and the absence of light.

- **White Light**: <u>reflection,</u> expression, manifestation, power

    o White is the absence of color and the dispeller of darkness.

    o Black light creates white light.

- Black light is the source of creation, where all things come from (pre-existence).

- White light is the reflection of all creation (the expression of creation in all of the manifested colors).

- From the darkness of the universe light descends into the darkness of the mind by entering the light of the pineal gland via the upper rear quadrant of the head. The light is then transferred into the darkness of the pituitary (master) gland. From the darkness of the pituitary gland, which distributes energy to all of the lower glands, light is emitted through the chakra body.

    - Healing hands emit light into the darkness of the body to create healing light that manifests after the session is complete.

Glandular Correspondences

Pineal	: Light assimilator	: Wisdom	Confusion
Pituitary	: Color regulator	: Illumination	Illusion
Thyroid	: Communication coordinator	: Truth	Falsehood
Thymus	: Heart of the spirit	: Love	Hate
Pancreas	: Life animator	: Comfort	Struggle
Sex glands	: Creator	: Desire	Rejection
Adrenal	: Staff of life	: Fight or	Flight

Keys to Channeling Reiki

- One should stay open to receiving energy (willing and accepting).
- One should not leak the energy (be able to receive in order to give).
- One should not try to control the healing environment or take the healing too seriously.
- Reiki is universal energy given out and regulated by the source of all there is.
- Control leads to stagnation and reduces one's connection.

Power: Energy formed by the intention of one's spirit is light (knowledge, wisdom and understanding) shaped by love and compassion and guided by conscious wisdom.

Choice Directs Power!

A Means to Awakening Spiritual Light

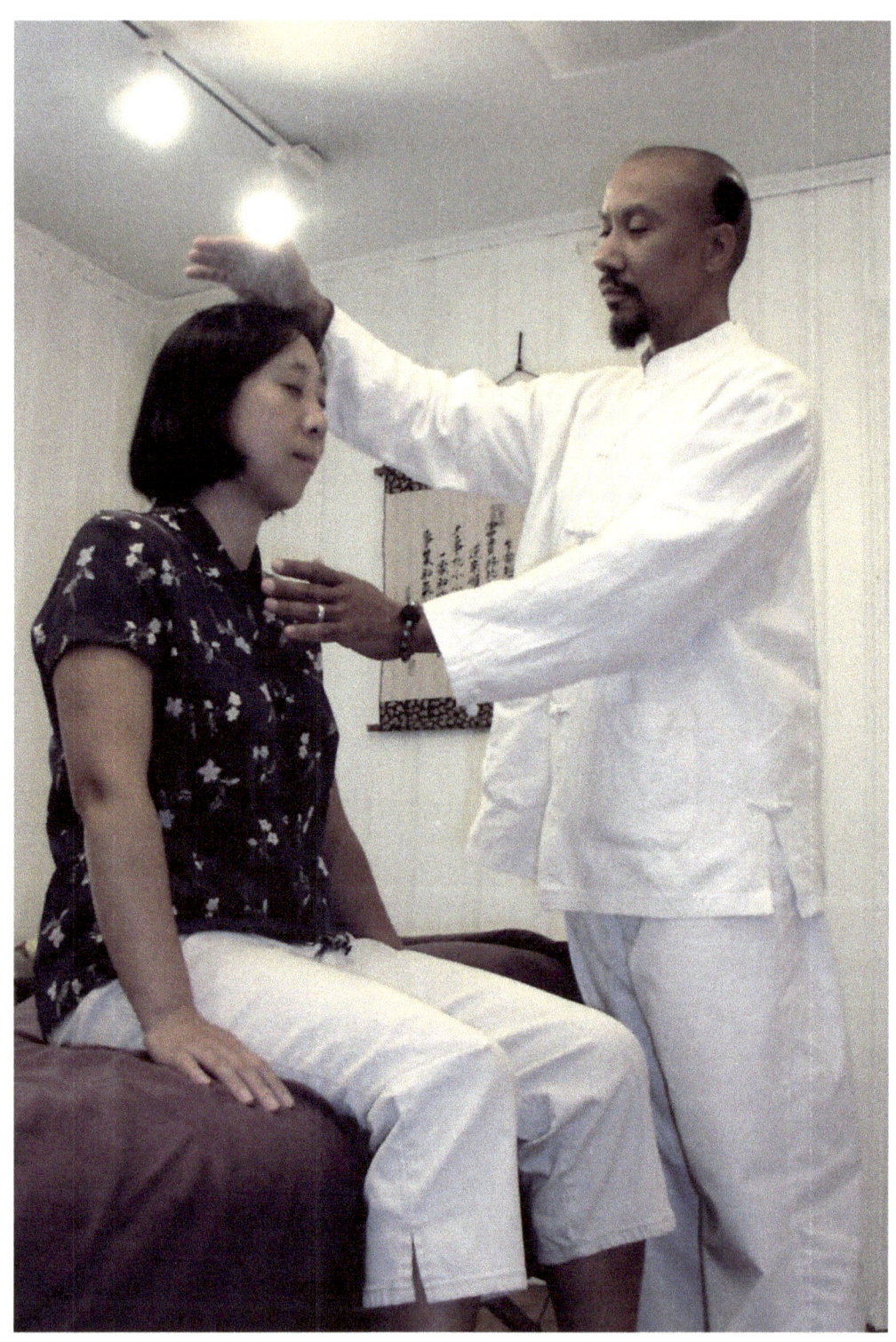

A Means to Awakening Spiritual Light

Self-Healing Circuit

1. Sit comfortably.
2. Place your vertical palms over your eyes.
3. Place your palms on the sides of your head with your middle fingers touching the crown of your head.
4. Place your vertical palms at the base of your skull.
5. Place your fingers over the back of your trapezius.
6. Place the backs of your palms over the heart chakra on your back (left hand above the right).
7. Place your palms over your kidney region with your middle fingers touching.
8. Place your palms over your sacrum in the shape of a "V" with your fingers pointing downward and touching.
9. Place your middle fingers on your perineum, with your left hand entering from the front and your right hand entering from the back.
10. Place your palms over your inguinal region in the shape of a "V" with your fingers touching.
11. Place your palms horizontally over your waist and insert your middle fingers into your naval region.
12. Place your palms over the ridge of your ribcage with your middle fingers meeting at the center of the base of your sternum.
13. Place your palms horizontally over your nipple region with your middle fingers meeting at the center of your sternum.
14. Place the heels of your palms together and place them over your throat region with your fingers pointing to the back of your neck.
15. Seal the treatment by inserting your two index fingers into the soft palette region below your chin.

*At each hand position, apply the 3.3.6.3. Breath for the count of four breathing cycles before moving on to the next hand position.

Cho Ku Rei

Power Symbol　　　　　　　　　　　　　　　　*Physical Body*

The Cho Ku Rei symbol is Tibetan with a mixture of Indian Sanskrit. The circular shape represents a conch shell and symbolizes calling to the heavens. Seven (7) is a consonant in the Tibetan alphabet, namely the tenth consonant. The Cho Ku Rei symbol directs and focuses power toward the physical body and penetrates through the spirit into the soul.

The Cho Ku Rei symbol represents primordial energy, the beginning; the essence of manifestation and the window of formless energy. It calls in the energy of the universe to increase the power of the treatment and issues forth the divine command that ensures the actualization of manifesting the request. It ***creates a solid platform*** (foundation) for the instantaneous appearance of the creative force of all existence.

The Cho Ku Rei symbol is considered the power symbol and voice of command that sets energies into motion to accomplish a desired task. The reversed symbol manifests the will of the receiver; it expands and magnifies the spiritual forces at your command and fills the void. The traditional symbol is used to remove blockages, pull out negative energies and perform psychic surgery.

The Cho Ku Rei symbol means "Put the spiritual power here" or "Fill this space with the manifestation of spiritual power."

The Cho Ku Rei symbol penetrates at a right angle and expands the energy in a spiral form. Right angles create a complete breakdown of the energy configuration. The seven is drawn vertically and the spiral is drawn horizontally. Use this symbol,

A Means to Awakening Spiritual Light

Cho Ku Rei, after drawing the Raku Rei (see on page 54) symbol to conduct the Cho Ku Rei's energy and increase its power.

- Used to increase energy and manifestation and direct power
- Primarily used with the physical body

The word "Cho" means : curved sword / curving movement
The word "Ku" means   : penetrating
The word "Rei" means : spirit and the soul

Attributes of the Cho Ku Rei symbol:

Color	Visualize in Violet
Body Region	Feet (hold for 5 minutes)
	Traditional, Reversed then Cho Ku Rei Staff
Gemstone	Blue/Yellow Topaz or Lapis Lazuli at the feet

Symbol Attunements

To receive your Traditional Cho Ku Rei symbol attunement please sit with your palms facing up on your lap and recite the following:

"Higher Self, I now accept the Traditional Cho Ku Rei symbol attunement prepared for me by Kiel Aman."

Traditional

To receive your Reversed Cho Ku Rei symbol attunement please sit with your palms facing up on your lap and recite the following:

"Higher Self, I now accept the Reversed Cho Ku Rei symbol attunement prepared for me by Kiel Aman."

Reversed

A Means to Awakening Spiritual Light

To receive your Bi-Polar Cho Ku Rei Staff symbol attunement please sit with your palms facing up on your lap and recite the following:

"Higher Self, I now accept the Bi-Polar Cho Ku Rei Staff symbol symbol attunement prepared for me by Kiel Aman."

To receive your Phat (sounds like "pate") symbol attunement please sit with your palms facing up on your lap and recite the following:

"Higher Self, I now accept the Phat symbol attunement prepared for me by Kiel Aman."

Healing With the Cho Ku Rei Symbol

Give the command of your intentions to direct the expansive energies, while invoking the power symbol using the following key:

- *The will to accomplish*
- *The desire to succeed*
- *The spoken word to actualize*

The above combination unites the physical energies with the spiritual energies to bring about manifestation.

Mantra of Spiritual Power:

"Om Ah Hum Vajra Guru Padma Siddhi Hum"

This mantra is uniquely powerful in that it can be used for the benefit of peace, healing, transformation and protection.

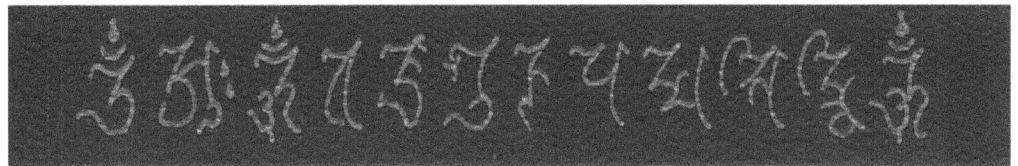

The "Cho Ku Rei" Symbol Invocations

(1) **Traditional: Removes deviant energies**
"*Cho Ku Rei, with a curving movement, you penetrate the spirit and soul. Put the spiritual power here. You are the one who has the power to remove all deviant energies. Expand (name) power to remove all deviant energies.*"

Om Ah Hum Vajra Guru Padma Siddhi Hum Phat!

(2) **Reversed: Removes weaknesses**
"*Cho Ku Rei, with a curving movement, you penetrate the spirit and soul. Fill this space with the manifestation of spiritual power. You are the one who increases the power to overcome all weaknesses. Expand (name) power to overcome all weaknesses.*"

Om Ah Hum Vajra Guru Padma Siddhi Hum!

(3) **Bi-polar Staff: Profound healing**
"*Cho Ku Rei, with a curving movement, you penetrate the spirit and soul. Put the spiritual power here and fill this space with its manifestation.*"

Om Ah Hum Vajra Guru Padma Siddhi Hum Phat Svaha!

Treatment: This treatment form is used to disperse pain syndromes and increase a person's healing capacity.

Invoke and then draw the Traditional Cho Ku Rei symbol. Move your hands over the affected area in a counter clockwise circular pattern to disrupt the energy field, while reciting the mantra approximately 27x, which will disperse any stagnant energy.

Invoke and then draw the Reversed Cho Ku Rei symbol. Move your hands over the affected area in a clockwise circular pattern to disrupt the energy field, while reciting the mantra approximately 27x, which will heal.

Draw and then invoke the Cho Ku Rei Staff; while holding your hands over the affected area and reciting the mantra until you feel a calming shift in the energy.

A Means to Awakening Spiritual Light

Cho Ku Rei Bi-Polar Staff Healing Techniques

The Friction: *Used to loosen stagnant or trapped energy by slowly moving your hands forward and backward as if rubbing something*

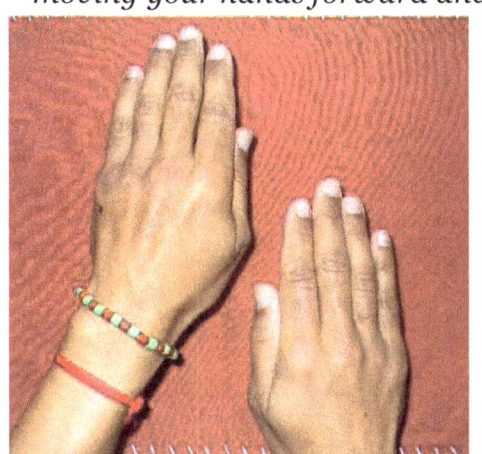
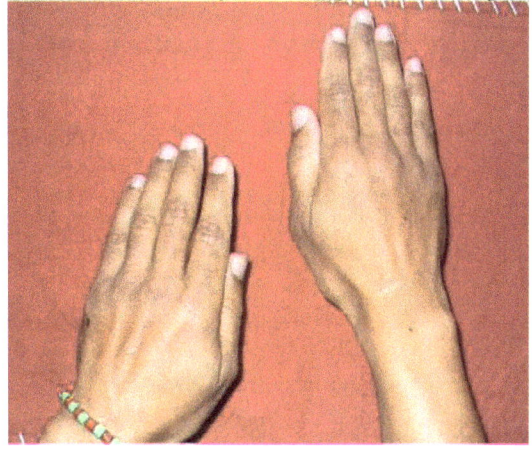

The Wash: *Used to stimulate movement by slowly flipping your palms over repeatedly*

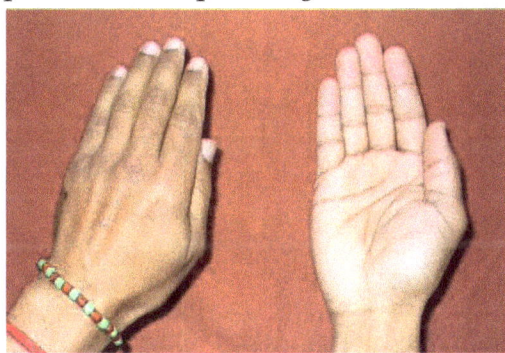
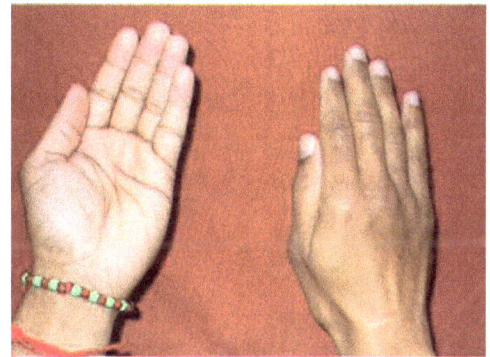

The Slinky: *Used to loosen stagnant or trapped energy by repeatedly move your palms up and down as if weighing Something*

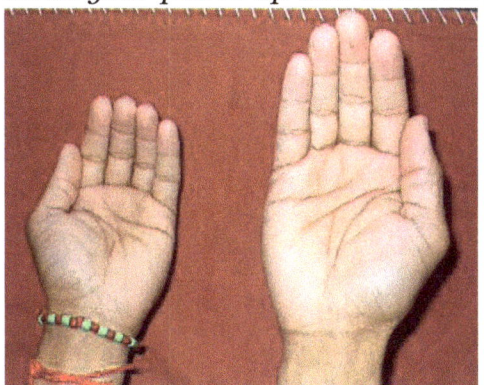
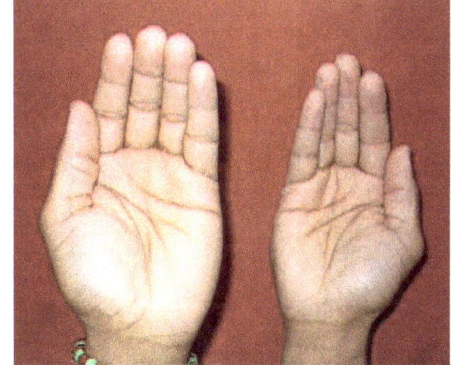

A Means to Awakening Spiritual Light

Triangle of Life Force *(Use Reversed Cho Ku Rei Symbol)*

Have the client lie face down:

1. Place your palms on both of the client's feet.

2. Place your right palm on the client's right foot and your left palm on the client's coccyx.

3. Place your right palm on the client's left foot and your left palm on the client's coccyx.

4. Place your right palm on the client's coccyx and your left hand gently presses the tip of the Earth (baby) finger.

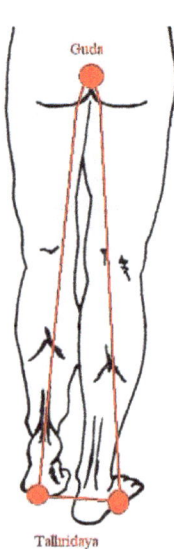

The Five Principles of Reiki:
The Virtues of Improving Your Character

Just for today, I will exhibit my trust (no harmful misconduct): Trying and trusting are mutually exclusive. One must choose to be connected to one's higher self by becoming focused on being connected.

Just for today, I will do all of my work honestly (no lying): Manipulation is the biggest form of disconnection.

Just for today, I will accept my many blessings (no stealing): If you cannot receive, then you cannot accept. Receiving is essential. A focus on good things creates good things.

Just for today, I will be at peace (no self-abuse): Let go of past memories and be connected to your center.

Just for today, I will respect the rights of all forms of life (no killing): Form creates spirit; each and every formed being carries the essence of life that we all share; in this connection, the spirit of life pervades the very existence of all living things. Therefore, in respecting all life forms you are in essence respecting yourself.

SECTION 2

Reiki Science

Eastern Science Reiki Categories
1. Ascending energy from the lower to the upper or the outer to the inner
2. Descending energy from the inner to the outer.

Reiki Components
1. The universe is you and all is inter-connected with the symbols.
2. You, universe and symbols: Without each other, they are not the same

Reiki Love Energy Polarity
1. Masculine love: Directs energies in the form of guidance and security
2. Feminine love: Directs energies in the form of nurturance and transformation.

There is orderliness to the Reiki system. When all of the components are used correctly, it always works. However, when one or more of the components are out of balance, the efficiency is not the same and, at times, will be nil.

Reiki a Universal Science of Energy
Reiki is a universal science of energy with the following characteristics:

- Endurance
- Stability
- Accumulative
- Harmlessness

- Sustaining power
- Expansive
- Operates from where you are to the beyond

The Reiki symbols radiate from within and focus intrinsically throughout the body utilizing etheric matrix force fields. The vibration of Reiki passes through the hands and eyes. It applies higher energies to the denser energy of the afflicted in order to uplift the density starting from the inner wholeness to the outer particular.

Healing with Reiki Energy

Universal Life Energy

Use your intuition, follow your impressions and go with your instincts even if you think they may seem strange. Healing is a joint effort. The person channeling Reiki energy and the person receiving the energy share in a cooperative healing effort. This healing effort is intrinsically focused into the person receiving the channeling; since the energy is flowing through the channeler; the channeler will also receive a residual healing from the exchange. In spite of appearances, on the physical level, the soul/spirit accepts only the highest and best for all concerned. This energetic acceptance through the soul/spirit may mean no physical signs of healing, but, on the etheric level, which cannot be seen with the naked eye, healing is always taking place.

Reiki energy knows what to do on its own. Healing comes from the intent. It always come from the "White Light" and always affirm that the highest and best action are happening. Never become attached to the outcome!

There is no right way or wrong way to perform a healing treatment. The energy is soul/universal life and knows what it is doing. You are just a channel for its expression. On the physical level, when you touch, you heal. When you take your hands off the client, the energy stops.

You are a receiving station to bring energy in to the world. A massive continual exchange of energy exists when you work on another body temple. The energy will always go where it is needed the most.

The law of attraction is: when someone comes to you, they want you! Perform the healing from your heart chakra. You are ready. You have done healings in your many past lifetimes. Trust and honor your inner guidance.

Channel energy one-to-one. Turn it over completely to the universe. You know nothing. Just allow it to happen. No rules!

Every person's temple is structured differently on the molecular level. The left side on most people is the receptive side and the right side is the expressive side.

Do not ever believe that nothing is happening as something is always happening. If you feel drained physically, emotionally or spiritually after giving a healing, then it is because you believe that you are performing the healing and not the energy. Do not try to control what is happening. Become unattached to the outcome. The person specifically being healed is the person receiving the energy, not the person channeling the energy.

Each healing session will be different and each person asking for healing will create what he needs.

Do not concentrate on what you are doing. Do not try to push or force the energy. When you try to manipulate the energy, the energy level drops. Keep your consciousness out of the energy channeling process. Accept the highest and best for all concerned.

You as the Reiki channeler wishing you were someplace else on the path can cause disease for yourself. Always remember, it is impossible for you to make a mistake with Reiki healings.

Remember: The body's suffering is a mask for what the mind is suffering.

Reiki is pronounced (ray kee) in the Japanese character system. Reiki is also "Ling Qi" in the Chinese character system. Both symbol systems are identical in the calligraphs as can be evidenced by checking any old Chinese dictionary. Both symbols originate from Tibet.

The Chinese interpretations of the Reiki symbol vary from the Japanese meanings. The top symbol Rei (Japanese) means spirit or soul. The Chinese (Ling) means subtle influences, the force, ethereal or supernatural power. The Tibetan source translates the symbols as the spirit of an entity that acts upon others and is supernatural, efficacious and clever.

A Means to Awakening Spiritual Light

Psychic Power Meditation

Step 1

1. Recite the full Traditional Cho Ku Rei invocation.
2. Visualize the Traditional Cho Ku Rei symbol at the 3rd eye.
3. Recite 12x the Vajra Guru Mantra of Removing Deviant Energies:

    'Om Ah Hum Vajra Guru Padma Siddhi Hum Phat!'

Note: Visualize the Traditional Cho Ku Rei symbol each time you recite the mantra and visualize the 'Phat' symbol superimposed over the Cho Ku Rei symbol at the completion of each recitation.

Traditional: Removes Deviant Energies
Cho Ku Rei, with a curving movement, you penetrate the spirit and soul. Put the spiritual power here. You are the one who has the power to remove all deviant energies. Expand (name) power to remove all deviant energies.

'Om Ah Hum Vajra Guru Padma Siddhi Hum Phat!'

Step 2

1. Recite the full Reversed Cho Ku Rei invocation.
2. Visualize the Reversed Cho Ku Rei symbol at the 3rd eye.
3. Recite 12x the Vajra Guru Mantra of Removing Weaknesses:

    'Om Ah Hum Vajra Guru Padma Siddhi Hum.'

A Means to Awakening Spiritual Light

Note: Visualize the Reversed Cho Ku Rei symbol each time you recite the mantra.

Reversed: Removes Weaknesses

Cho Ku Rei, with a curving movement, you penetrate the spirit and soul. Fill this space with the manifestation of spiritual power. You are the one who increases the power to overcome all weaknesses. Expand (name) power to overcome all weaknesses.

Om Ah Hum Vajra Guru Padma Siddhi Hum Phat.

Step 3

Recite: *"Cho Ku Rei, with a curving movement, you penetrate the spirit and soul,"* while visualizing the Bi-Polar Cho Ku Rei inside your head at the 3rd eye level.

Recite: *"Put the spiritual power here and fill this space with its manifestation,"* while visualizing the pole of the staff down your central channel to your perineum.

Recite the Vajra Guru Mantra of Profound Healing:

"Om Ah Hum Vajra Guru Padma Siddhi Hum Phat Svaha!"

While visualizing and uniting the Traditional and Reversed Cho Ku Rei symbols at their bases and visualizing the pole of the staff down through your central channel to your perineum. Finish by visualizing the "Phat" symbol at the top center of the Cho Ku Rei staff (as shown in the diagram below).

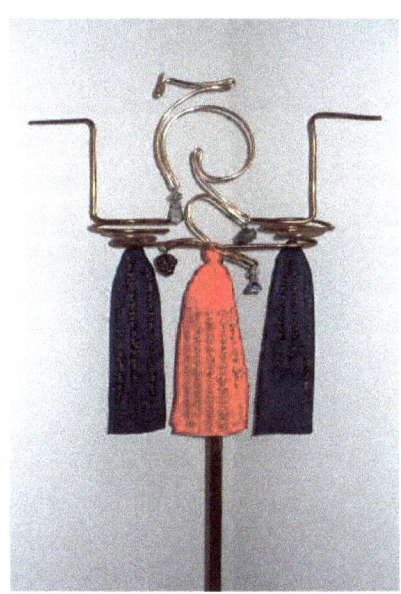

Sei He Ki

Protection Symbol   *Mental Body*

The Sei He Ki symbol originates from the Japanese culture and is used to bring the body into alignment. It balances and aligns the upper four chakras in order to improve mental, spiritual and emotional well-being.

The symbol represents man and spirit becoming one. It also represents the phrase "I have the key" as well as the integration of the mind, body and spirit. This symbol unlocks the subconscious mind. One may experience a past life recall when using this symbol. The Sei He Ki symbol offers protection from negative influences and it is effective in treating mental and emotional disturbances. This symbol increases emotional stability. The Sei He Ki symbol allows for transmutation and the relaxation of the mind. This symbol unblocks and releases trapped energies.

The Sei He Ki symbol consciously activates the higher spirit within via one's memory and emotions. The energy lasts and transforms over time. When using the Sei He Ki symbol, one must ground and direct one's intentions.

The word "Sei" means: The origin of the external form, which rises up into the internal form.

The word "He" means: Base chakra with the sense of being in a state of balance.

The word "Ki" means: energy that brings discordant energies into balance or manifestation.

The word "Hrih" means : To free oneself from all causes and effects (i.e., purifying all defilements, removing all delusions and dissolving all manifested and created forms).

Attunements

To receive your Sei He Ki symbol attunement please sit with your palms facing up on your lap and recite the following:

"Higher Self, I now accept the Sei He Ki symbol attunement prepared for me by Kiel Aman."

To receive your Sei He Ki Shield symbol attunement please sit with your palms facing up on your lap and recite the following:

"Higher Self, I now accept the Sei He Ki Shield symbol attunement prepared for me by Kiel Aman."

Creates the unfoldment of the flowering Lotus

- Used for protection, purification, cleansing and harmony
- Primarily used with the mind and emotions
- Makes one aware of the spirit
- Adds comfort due to the connection it makes with the spirit
- Used as a connector

Attributes of the Sei He Ki Symbol

Color   Visualize in Violet
Body region   Navel (hold for five minutes)
Gemstone   Place Herkimer Diamond at navel

Working with the Sei He Ki Symbol

Sealing the Room

Infinity Symbol Invocation:
Start in the prayer palms position

With the right hand circling counter-clockwise, recite:
"I ward off all negativity on the right hand side."

With the left hand circling clockwise, recite:
"I ward off all negativity on the left hand side."

With both hands circling outward recite twice:
"I am - all encompassing - in my thoughts, my deeds and my actions."

Bring your fingers to your third eye and then return to the prayer palms position at the heart center and recite:
"I am one with the light."

With your right hand, draw the Sei He Ki symbol toward one wall of the room. Recite the Sei He Ki invocation. Then, direct both palms toward the wall and hold for approximately one minute. Repeat for the remaining walls, ceiling and floor.

Cleansing the Head

Pour enough coconut milk to cover the top of your head. Then, do the same with cool water. Hold your hands on the top of your head. Invoke your guardian spirit to protect your mind and give you clarity and stability. Pray for what you desire and seal your head with the Se He Ki symbol. Recite the Se He Ki invocation. Cover your head with a white cloth or hat. Do not go outdoors until the next day.

Perform cleansing of the head during the
Spiritual Communion Time
7 p.m. to 9 p.m.

House Cleansing

- Burn one part myrrh resin to three parts frankincense resin (Attracts negative energies and dissolves them)
- Burn white sage to disperse negative energies
- Burn sweet grass to attract positive energies
  Or
- Burn amber to ground down the Buddha energy

Perform house cleansing during the
Spiritual Protection Time
9 p.m. to 11 p.m.

Candle Cleansing

Hold the candle with your non-dominant hand. Wipe the candle down with your dominant hand and throw the negative energies into the light of the universe, or you can throw it into a selenite crystal, salt water, etc. Empower the candle using the Se He Ki symbol and invocation. Place the candle at the head of the treatment area.

Taking a Cleansing Bath

1 Box Epsom Salt
3 drops of Myrrh essential oil
9 drops of Frankincense essential oil
1 container (2 gallon capacity)

Pour 1.5 gallons of hot water into the container and then pour the Epsom salts and essential oils into the container. Place the Se He Ki symbol into the container and recite the invocation.

Allow the mixture to sit for five to 10 minutes. Run a bath of lukewarm to cool water. Recite a prayer of your own removing all negativities that you may have accumulated since the last time you took a cleansing bath. Stand inside the tub and scoop out the salt mixture in small handfuls. Use these handfuls to wash your body from head to toe. Immerse your entire body in the tub water and soak for 20 minutes. Let the water drain from the tub completely before you get out. Recite seven times, while the water is draining *"I discharge all negativities I have accumulated into the water and down the drain."*

Cleansing the Treating Hands after Treatments

Place cool water and sea salt into a clear glass bowl. Place it at the foot of the treatment table. When you finish your treatment, place both of your hands into the water. Direct the negative energies into the water by reciting "I release all negativities I may have accumulated from this treatment into the water to be dissolved in the light of the universe."

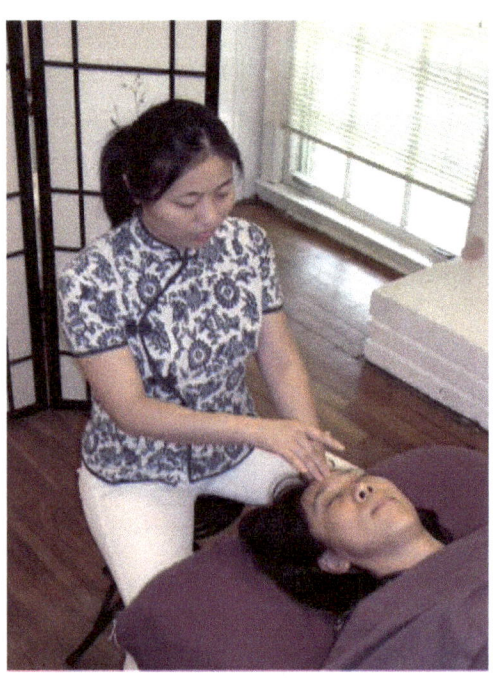

Sei He Ki Invocation

By the light of the North
By the peace of the South
By the illumination of the East
By the grace of the West
From the center of the heart from where you rest
You are shielded with 360 degrees by 360 degrees
by 360 degrees of white light
Sei He Ki (name), Sei He Ki (name), Sei He Ki (name)

"Hrih Symbol"

Om Mani Padme Hum *(I am a Spirit through and through)*

Note: The Sei He Ki Symbol is also the seed symbol "Hrih" from the mantra garland of Om Mani Padme Hum, which spiritually represents the proclaiming of the self (i.e., "I am Spirit through and through"). If a client asks the meaning of the words "Sei He Ki," you can tell the client it means "May the light of God be with you."

- *Hrih harmonizes the mind and emotions. It is the life force energy of the power of light.*
- *Hrih calls forth the power of the 'om mani padme hum' which is total compassion.'*

Attunement

To receive your Hrih symbol attunement please sit with your palms facing up on your lap and recite the following:

"Higher Self, I now accept the Hrih symbol attunement prepared for me by Kiel Aman."

Mental Clearing

Have your client lie face down on the therapy table and sit next to the right side of the client's head. Place your left hand horizontally over the back of your client's head and your right hand vertically over the crown of your clients head. Draw the Se He Ki symbol over the crown of your clients head and say the Se He Ki invocation. Maintain your hand positions until you feel a calmness overtake the palms of your hands; this is the actual clearing process. This calmness usually takes approximately five to 20 minutes to accomplish. You should mentally recite *"Om Mani Padme Hum"* during the mental clearing process.

Triangle of Emotions

1. Have your client lie on his or her back.
2. Place both of your hands on Urvi for three minutes.
3. Place your right hand on the left Urvi and place your left hand on the Vasti for three minutes.
4. Place your right hand and on the right Urvi and your left hand on the Vasti for three minutes.
5. Place your right hand on the Vasti, while your left hand holds your water finger. Hold this position for one minute.

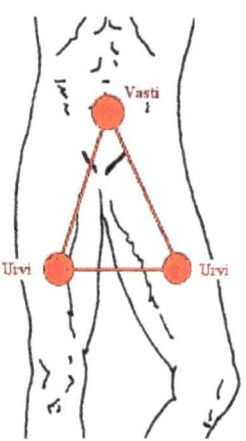

SECTION 3

Healing Hands Invocation

"My hands behold the essence of the light of purity and cures the ailments of all."

My hands	: the energies that I manifest through the
behold	: works of my being embraces and conducts
the essence	: the source derived from spiritual assistance
of the light	: knowledge, wisdom and understanding
of purity	: the unknown yet to be revealed or made manifest
and cures	: the means to heal
the ailments	
of all	: the afflictions of the mind, body, emotions

Chakra Meditation 7:1 Root 1:7

1. Sit comfortably on a small stool or chair in a quiet area of the house or outdoors.

2. Hold your head erect and your back straight. Rest your arms in your lap. Relax, clear your mind and close your eyes.

3. Focus your attention on the crown of your head (chakra 7). Feel the energy of the universe descend from the heavens into the crown and see the golden white light. Wait for the energy to pulsate.

4. After feeling the pulsation at the crown, shift your attention to the third eye (chakra 6). See the color violet and wait for the energy to pulsate.

5. After feeling the pulsation at the third eye, shift your attention to the throat center (chakra 5). See the color aquamarine and wait for the energy to pulsate.

6. After feeling the pulsation at the throat center, shift your attention to the heart center (chakra 4). See the color green and wait for the energy to pulsate.

7. After feeling the pulsation at the heart center, shift your attention to the pit of the upper abdomen (chakra 3). See the color yellow and wait for the energy to pulsate

8. After feeling the pulsation in the pit of the upper abdomen, shift your attention to the area just below the navel (chakra 2). See the color orange and wait for the energy to pulsate.

9. After feeling the pulsation in the area just below the navel, shift your attention to the coccyx area (chakra 1). See the color red and wait for the energy to pulsate.

10. After feeling the pulsation in the coccyx area, imagine two cords with anchoring devices attached to their ends traveling deep into the core of the Earth and then anchoring in the Earth. Feel the energy from the core of the Earth rise up the cords and into the coccyx, energizing it.

11. Imagine one cord attached to each hip traveling down through the legs and soles of the feet into the Earth until these cords reach the core and anchor there. Feel the energy from the core of the Earth rise up the cords until it reaches the hips and the earth's core energy unites at the coccyx.

12. Feel the energy fed by the Earth germinate into the first chakra and see the color red.

13. After feeling the pulsation in chakra one, draw the energy up into chakra two. See the color orange and wait for the pulsation.

14. After feeling the pulsation in chakra two, draw the energy up into chakra three. See the color yellow and wait for the pulsation.

15. After feeling the pulsation in chakra three, draw the energy up into chakra four. See the color green and wait for the pulsation.

16. After feeling the pulsation in chakra four, draw the energy up into chakra five. See the color aquamarine and wait for the pulsation.

17. After feeling the pulsation in chakra five, draw the energy up into chakra six. See the color violet and wait for the pulsation.

18. After feeling the pulsation in chakra six, draw the energy up into chakra seven. See the color golden-white and wait for the pulsation.

19. After feeling the pulsation in the seventh chakra; Sit for a few minutes to allow the energy to settle back into its original state.

Raku Rei

Anchors the Spirit *Spiritual Body*

The Magnetic Attraction Symbol Raku Rei

Invocation

*I believe in the great cosmic magnet that
manifest as the spirit of truth, love and light.
This cosmic magnet lives in you
as part of your divine nature.
You recognize the pure white light in your soul.
This divine spirit in your soul continually
guides you in all that you think, say and do.
Through your magnetic personality, (name),
you impart your divine essence into the world
As you give, so shall you receive,
living happily,
expressing creatively
and experiencing the perfection of well-being.
So be it now and forever.*

Attunement

To receive your Raku Rei symbol attunement please sit with your palms facing up on your lap and recite the following:

"Higher Self, I now accept the Raku Rei symbol attunement prepared for me by Kiel Aman."

To receive your Raku Phat symbol attunement please sit with your palms facing up on your lap and recite the following:

"Higher Self, I now accept the Raku Phat symbol attunement prepared for me by Kiel Aman."

 ***The Raku Rei symbol conducts the Cho Ku Rei symbol*** *by the channel drawing the Raku symbol in the air and upon touching down to the floor/ground immediately draw the Phat symbol (the Siddham Sanskrit version of the Cho Ku Rei), which is used to emphasize, conduct and expand electro-magnetic power.*

Hung *is the Tibetan pronunciation of the Sanskrit term* **Hum***, which is the seed sound for the Vishuddha (throat) chakra. This seed sound is quite powerful in regard to repelling unwanted vibrations.*

The **Vajra** *thunderbolt indicates the power of the mind to penetrate any environment (material, physical, mental or emotional).*

Pay *is the Tibetan pronunciation for the Sanskrit term* **Phat***, another seed sound that repels unwanted energy.*

A sphere of consciousness surrounds our planet. Within this sphere are destructive forces that are sometimes called thought-forms. These packages of negative energy, which are created by anger, violence, terrible events (like world wars) and other ignominious aspects of consciousness, cause havoc every day. Circulating like blobs of oil within the ocean of consciousness, these bits of gunk need to be neutralized in some way.

Hum Vajra Phat! *(Spiritually cleanses a room, space or one's personal aura of all evils, negativities and harmful energy.)*

Chant this mantra "Hum Vajra Phat" *to cleanse the negative energy of the Earth's layer of consciousness.*

A Means to Awakening Spiritual Light

The Raku Rei symbol grounds down from the sky white light energy from the fifth dimension through the seven chakra. This symbol grounds down conscious thought (chakra 7), which allows for intuitive insight (chakra 6). Intuitive sight allows for the manifestation of vibrational sound patterns (chakra 5), which create new realities through the acceptance of change within the evolving spirit (chakra 4). This acceptance gives rise to newfound power (chakra 3) and allows for feelings to be expressed (chakra 2), which brings about the manifestation of the divine will (chakra 1).

- Used in grounding and anchoring the light of the spirit
- Used in purifying the energy matrix of the body and mind
- Shatters and cleanses stagnant energy fields
- Primarily used for specific pinpoint energy focuses

Attributes of the Raku Rei

Color Visualize in Violet
Body region Crown (hold for five minutes)
Gemstone Place Fulgurite at the crown of your head

Treatment note: *When a person is feeling spacey or ungrounded, have that person lie on his back and then invoke the Raku Rei. Place the symbol and both hands at the crown of the head and hold that position for three to five minutes. When finished, seal the person's head with the Sei He Ki symbol. You may, if you like, recite the "Om mani padme hum" mantra as well.*

To Cleanse Negativity from the Environment:
Use the Hum Mudra (hand formation), while reciting **Hum Vajra**. *Clap your hands and recite* **Phat**. *Repeat as many times as you feel necessary. You will know when to stop by feeling a shift of energy within the environment you are in.*

Working with the Raku Rei

Adrenal Treatment

Check to see if the client suffers from adrenal exhaustion by placing your fingers at the client's vertical midline above the navel and pressing toward the therapy table. If you feel a strong pulse, then it is possible that the client suffers from adrenal exhaustion.

For confirmation: Place your thumb at the five o'clock position on the outer rim of the navel and press toward the therapy table. Then, press toward the center of the navel. Do the same at the seven o'clock position. If you feel the client's pulse or the client winces in slight pain, then adrenal exhaustion has been confirmed.

The treatment: Have the client lie in the supine position and stand to their right side. Locate **Kidney 6** (at the base of the ankle) and **Kidney 27** (at the origin of the collarbone at the first rib space); Draw and recite the Raku Rei symbol and invocation over the two acu-points by placing you index fingers cross body at the left ankle region and the right collarbone region. Hold your position until you feel a change or balancing in the energy between the two points. Then, switch sides.

Ether Element:
Balancing the Two Hemispheres of the Brain

Have the client lie in the supine position, while you sit at the head of the table. Draw and recite the Raku Rei symbol and invocation over the third eye center. Then, place the fingers of your left hand on the left side of the client's head, with your thumb at the top of the crown of the client's head. Place your right ring and middle fingers on the third eye and hold until you feel a change in the energy. Switch the position of your hands and repeat on the other side of the client's body.

A Means to Awakening Spiritual Light

Powerful Prayer to Bring Forth Evil

It is the truth that brings forth the wisdom of the ages.

It is the light of being that is repressed within that hall of the ages.

Let the truth shineth upon the land.

True expression come forth into the light of being.

Come forth! Come forth! Come forth!

(Then, recite the great Hebrew mantra below to dissolve the evil.)

Powerful Universal Hebrew Mantra (Sacred Words)
Sacred words for warding off evils and increasing vibrations to their highest level

"Ka-dosh, Ka-dosh, Ka-dosh, Ah-do-noi, Sa-bay-ot"
Holy, Holy, Holy, Is the Lord God of Hosts

The vibration of the Kadosh mantra can help open the way for your Guardian Angel and all other Beings of Light that you *personally acknowledge to come to your aid. The Kadoish mantra is extremely powerful in regard to clearing the electro-magnetic fields of the body. It can be used as a bridge to access other dimensions. It is sacred and can be used for protection of the self and family to deter the Dark Brotherhood.*

"I ask the powerful spiritual guides to remove any possessing entities from my or (person's name) being."

"Spiritual Guide, please remove any blockages to my or (person's name) higher self as well as any implants, negative thought forms, hexes, curses or harmful spells and turn them into Universal Light."

"Spiritual Guide, please consume, dissolve and transmute all negative energy, thought forms and poisons left by the implants from discarnate entities and allow them to dissolve. Cut all cords back to their sources."

SECTION 4

Kanji

Kanji: Hand Positions for Centering and Balance
The kanji are used to influence the reception of spiritual energies into and through the body/mind continuum. They can be used prior to giving treatments, when undertaking meditation or just when looking for answers.

Kanji 1
Interlace your fingers with your index fingers pointing upward. Keep your eyes closed and focus on your spiritual heart center (chakra 4) for about 30 seconds, while envisioning a deep blue light. This kanji is used to center the mind and bring in spiritual energy. Recite in your mind:

"I choose to be that I am. I am the multi-dimensional integrated light being (your name)."

Kanji 2
Interlace your fingers with your middle fingers pointing upward. Keep your eyes closed and focus on your spiritual heart center (chakra 4) for three minutes, while envisioning a radiant white light. This kanji is used to fill the body with light (knowledge, wisdom and understanding) embody spiritual energy. Recite in your mind:

"I know that I am; I am the multi-dimensional integrated light being (your name)."

Kanji 3
This kanji is the kanji of confidence and knowing. Start by interlocking your fingers with all of your fingers pointing upward. Keep your eyes closed and focus on the spiritual heart center (chakra 4). The maintaining of this focus will get you to enter into

an alpha state of consciousness. Upon entering into an alpha state, recite in your mind,

"All that is, I am that I am. I am the multi-dimensional integrated light being (your name)." Then, add, *"I wish to know the true cause of (a particular affliction)"* or *" I wish to know the truth about (a particular thing)"* and wait for the answer.

After a bit of practice, the answers will come increasingly quickly. This practice is well worth the time and effort spent to acquire its (result of the practice) essence. Remember to trust your instincts and that your first impression is usually the correct answer. Trust in the communication with the spirit.

Kanji 1

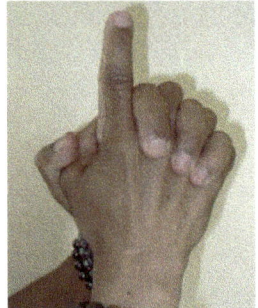

Kanji 2

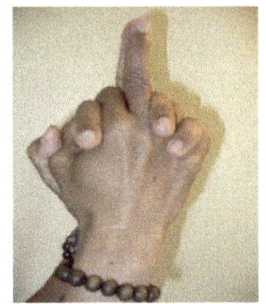

Kanji 3

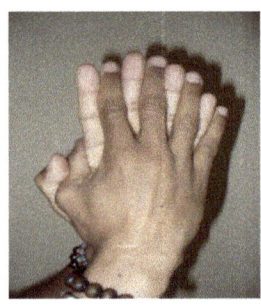

A Means to Awakening Spiritual Light

Standard Reiki Healing Sequence

Supine Massage ear rims and lobes, eye orbits and nose bridge
        Palms over eyes   (Raku Rei, Cho Ku Rei)
        Palms over ears   (Raku Rei, Cho Ku Rei)

Prone Mental clearing   (Raku Rei, Cho Ku Rei, Sei He Ki)
        Palms over crown   (Raku Rei, Cho Ku Rei)
        Palms over occiput   (Raku Rei, Cho Ku Rei)
        Pyramid palms over throat   (Raku Rei, Cho Ku Rei)
        Palms across upper back   (Raku Rei, Cho Ku Rei, Sei He Ki)
        Palms across mid back   (Raku Rei, Cho Ku Rei)
        Palms across waist   (Raku Rei, Cho Ku Rei, Sei He Ki)
        Alternate palms over sacrum   (Raku Rei, Cho Ku Rei, Sei He Ki)
        Fingers locked, pointing toward perineum   (Raku Rei, Cho Ku Rei)

Supine Alternate palms over inguinal region   (Raku Rei, Cho Ku Rei, Sei He Ki)
        Palms across naval   (Raku Rei, Cho Ku Rei, Sei He Ki)
        Palms across ribcage border   (Raku Rei, Cho Ku Rei)
        Palms across breast   (Raku Rei, Cho Ku Rei, Sei He Ki)
        Pyramid palms over throat   (Raku Rei, Cho Ku Rei)
        Fingers locked into soft palette   (Raku Rei, Cho Ku Rei)

Left Shoulder and Hand Connection:

Cradle the shoulder, elbow, wrist and palms   (Raku Rei, Cho Ku Rei).
Pull the energy out from the hands
Repeat on the right side

Five Element Finger Connections:

Gently pinch and hold the elemental sets
of fingers in the following order   (Earth element – baby fingers)
        (Water element – ring fingers)
        (Fire element – middle fingers)
        (Air element – index fingers)
        (Ether element—thumbs)

Left Hip and Foot Connection:

Cradle hip, knee, ankle and foot sole   (Raku Rei, Cho Ku Rei)
Pull the energy out from the toes
Repeat on the right side

Five Element Foot Connections:

Grasp and pop each toe joint
Gently pinch and hold the elemental
Sets of toes in the following order   (Ether element – big toes)
    (Air element – index toes)
    (Fire element – middle toes)
    (Water element – ring toes)
    (Earth element—baby toes)

Sweep the entire body

A Means to Awakening Spiritual Light

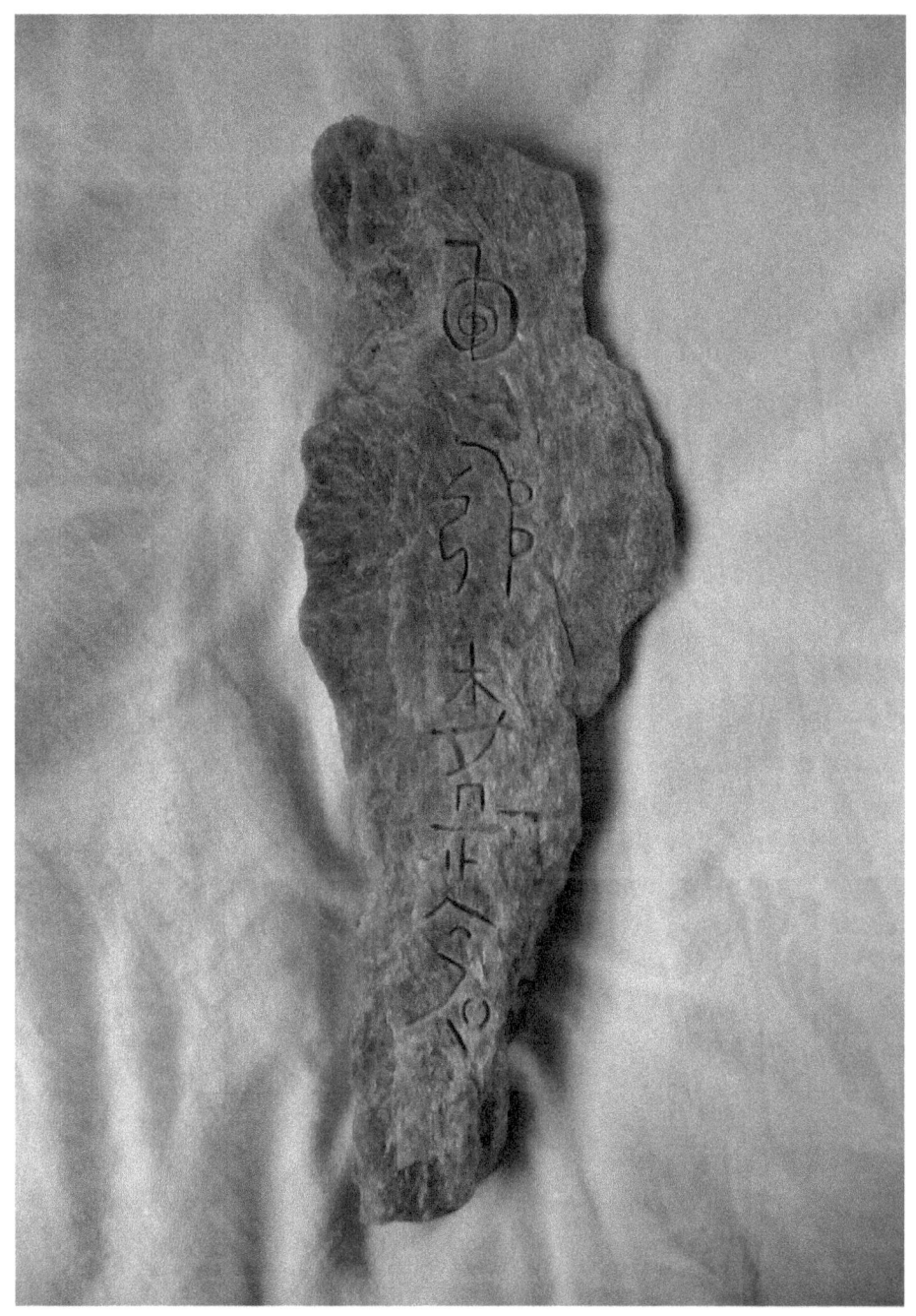

"Reiki Lineage Tremolite Staff"

A Means to Awakening Spiritual Light

Psychic Shield Meditation

- Recite the Sei He Ki invocation:

By the light of the North,
By the peace of the South,
By the illumination of the East,
By the grace of the West,
From the center of the heart from where you rest,
You are shielded with 360 degrees, by 360 degrees,
By 360 degrees of pure white protective light.

- Visualize the Sei He Ki Shield symbol inside the body at the heart center in front of the spine and recite:

"This is the secret shield of all protection."

- Then recite:

"Om Mani Padme Hum Hrih."

- After saying Hrih at the end of the mantra, visualize the Hrih symbol superimposed over the Sei He Ki shield. This action completes one cycle. Repeat this process for 12 cycles.

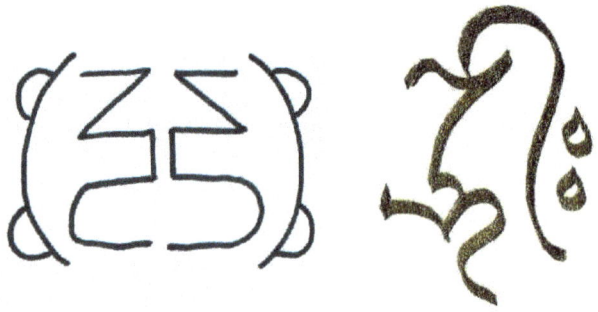

SECTION 5

Hon Sha Zah Sho Nen
Symbol of the Cosmic Stupa

Distant Healing Symbol   *Light of the Emotional Body*

The Hon Sha Zah Sho Nen symbol is Chinese. This symbol is the master key to the secrets Reiki, known only to some masters. The top third is related to, on or under something and also to a person with a smile. The next third is related to living and food. The bottom third is a highly stylized form of writing related to the bridge between two worlds. This symbol is the "ether tube" connection used to send distant healing energy to those individuals in need, wherever they may be.

The Hon Sha Zah Sho Nen symbol means "I bestow the truth of truths upon you" and "the Buddha within me reaches out to the Buddha within you to bestow enlightenment and peace." This symbol is the power of the universe moving beyond idea or separation to where an immediate connection in oneness exists.

Healing takes place within the oneness and the presence of the "Mighty I am." This symbol is used in distant healing and is the only symbol that is in calligraphy.

The Hon Sha Zah Sho Nen symbol represents the compassionate heart. The expansion and contraction of love, oneness with the love of all, Wu Chi (supreme emptiness), five life sources or valves of the heart, and the central core that balances good and evil. This symbol is literally the spiritual heart of Reiki as it creates a bridge between two worlds, opening closed doors and closing open doors. It contains all of the mind forms of the five Buddha Families of the three times (past, present and future) that embody the holy stupa.

Namaste: An East Indian expression meaning *"My spirit reaches out to your spirit."*

A Means to Awakening Spiritual Light

The **Hon Sha Zah Sho Nen** symbol activates one's spiritual path, uncovers the master within and is the connection that draws love to you.

本	Ben	Original
有	You	Has
正	Zheng	Correct
念	Nian	Mind

Meaning:

"*Originally having the Correct (Buddhic) Mind,*"

Attributes of the Hon Sha Zah Sho Nen Symbol

Color   Visualize in Violet
Body Region   Sternum (hold for five minutes)
Gemstone   Place Sugilite at sternum

Creates the moon disk
(symbol of the reflection of the light of the sun)

- Used for spiritual growth
- Primarily used in distance healing
- Use in conjunction with the Dai Koo Myo symbol
- Heals past/present/future karma

Calligraphic and Siddham Sanskrit version of the Hon Sha Zah Sho Nen symbol seen below are used as talismans to help dissolve unwanted contact with souls of the deceased. They are the barrier that separates humans from spirits.

Note: refer to the numbered sequence of the Hon Sha Zah Sho Nen symbol for the below number references.

Hon (1-5) Source, central essence, wholeness beyond any idea or parts
Effort Focusing of Energies
Compassion of the heart, heart of the hearts, central core (to unite)

Sha (6-11) Shimmering aspect of light, balance between the emotional and mental
Mindfulness Active state of awareness
Light of the heart (love), Emotional heart (to regulate)

Zah (12-15) Advancing, going forward on a correct course
Concentration Single-point of focus
Soul of the heart, allows for the enlightenment and growth of the soul (to move ahead)

Sho (16-18) Target, shimmering essence, represents integrity and becoming an honest being
Faith Trust and confidence
Truth of the heart, the magnetic attraction of the spirit (to seek out)

Nen (19-22) Thought before expression
Wisdom Intuitive understanding
Spirit of the heart, etheric heart, the true heart of feeling where the memories are stored and recorded (thought before action)

A Means to Awakening Spiritual Light

Hon Sha Zah Sho Invocation

The universe is filled with power and mysteries.
I am the magnetic attraction of the light of life
He who has the power of healing hands,
power comes.
Just as I summon the healing power,
I am given the power.
My hands behold the essence of the light of purity
And completely cure everyone they touch.
When my hands stretch forth,
They heal with light, love and power.
"Hon Sha Zah Sho Nen"
You are the one who opens closed doors.
You are the one who closes open doors.
Open the doorway to releasing blockages.
Close the doorway to sealing leakages
May the love of the one soul radiate upon you,
(person's name),
And permeate every part of your body,
Healing, soothing, strengthening and dissipating
All that hinders service and good health.

Attunements

To receive your Hon Sha Zah Sho Nen symbol attunement please sit with your palms facing up on your lap and recite the following:

"Higher Self, I now accept the Hon Sha Zah Sho Nen symbol attunement prepared for me by Kiel Aman."

A Means to Awakening Spiritual Light

To receive your Vai symbol attunement please sit with your palms facing up on your lap and recite the following:

"Higher Self, I now accept the Vai symbol attunement prepared for me by Kiel Aman."

Vairocana 15 Syllable Mantra of the Cosmic Stupa
Creates the Body of Light, The Body of the Buddha (Enlightened Being)

Protruding Siddhi: A Ra Pa Ca Na: Christ Self

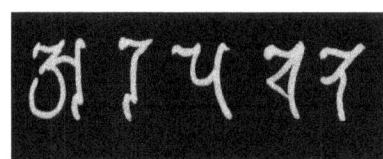

This section of the mantra generates roots and stems and permeates the four directions. It frees you from all troubles and sufferings. It eliminates all major sins committed over 100 million eons of rebirths and surrounds and protects you. It travels from the feet to the waist.

Intruding Siddhi: A Vi Ra Hum Kham: I Am Presence

This section of the mantra generates branches and leaves. Its bright light penetrates the triple realms. It is an adamantine formula for the subjugation of the four classes of demons, the six elements (earth, water, fire, wind, ether and the deity) and the attainment of universal wisdom. It travels from the navel to the heart. The five letters here represent the material elements.

Upper Siddhi: A Vam Ram Ham Kham: Causal Body

This section of the mantra is of the cosmic stupa, secret siddhi and dharmadhatu secret words to attain Buddhahood and experience Bodhi. Its light permeates everywhere and travels from the heart to the top of the head.

Working with the Hon Sha Zah Sho Nen Symbol

Sit in a quiet place where you will not be easily distracted and then perform the Great Invocation.

1

From the point of light within the mind of my ascended spirit,
Let Light stream forth into the mind of (name).
Let Light descend into my body.

2

From the point of Love within the Heart of my luminous soul, Let Love stream forth into the heart of (name).
May the spiritual light of my luminous soul unite in oneness with me.

3

From the center where the will of the spirit of my soul is known,
Let purpose guide the little will of (name),
The purpose which the Masters know and serve.

4

From the center which we call the race of men, Let the Plan of Love and Light work out and may it seal the door where evil dwells.

Let Light, Love and Power restore the Plan within me.

Spiritual guide invocation:

"O Spiritual Guide, *open the path to healing using me as* *a channel."*

Distant Healing

Sit in a comfortable position. Use a photograph, think of the person's name or hold the intention of the person in your mind. Then, cup your left hand under your naval and place your right hand with the palm facing outward in front of your chest. State your intentions of who you are and why you are sending distance healing. With your right hand, invoke and draw the traditional Cho Ku Rei symbol, Se He Ki symbol and Hon Sha Zah Sho Nen symbol. Focus both palms at the object of your intentions and send the healing energies.

Embodiment of Light: Invoking the Christ Self

Have the client lie on table in the supine position. Invoke the Hon Sha Zah Sho Nen symbol and then draw the symbol using your right hand placed at the bladder region just below the navel. With your left hand, grasp client's ring finger. Visualize the "**A Ra Pa Ca Na**" Siddham symbols in golden violet light. Repeat the visualization seven more times.

Embodiment of Light: Invoking the I Am Presence

Have the client lie on the table in the supine position. Invoke the Hon Sha Zah Sho Nen symbol and then draw the symbol using your right hand placed at the heart center. With your left hand, grasp clients index finger. Visualize the **A Vi Ra Hum Kham** Siddham symbols in golden violet light. Repeat the visualization seven more times.

Embodiment of Light: Invoking the Causal Self

Have the client lie on the table in the supine position. Invoke the Hon Sha Zah Sho Nen symbol and then draw symbol using both hands placed at the crown center. Visualize the **A Vam Ram Ham Kham** Siddham symbols in golden violet light. Repeat the visualization seven more times.

A Means to Awakening Spiritual Light

Triangle of Force (To re-activate the Life force from a state of depression)

1. Have the client lie in the supine position.
2. Place both of your thumbs on the Manubrium.
3. Place your left middle finger
4. Place your right middle finger on the right Stanyarohita.

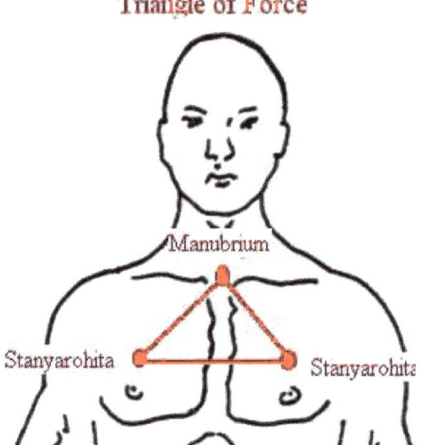

Attuning to the Reiki Symbol
1. Sit in a comfortable position.
2. Place your prayer palms in front of the third eye region.
3. Invoke the particular symbol that you wish to extract information from.
4. Ask the symbol to teach you the secrets to its power.
5. Draw the symbol with your third eye.
6. Open your palms in front of your third eye and meditate on the symbol.

SECTION 6

Dai Koo Myo Master Symbol

Initiation   *Light of the Spirit and Soul Body*

What is a Master?

A master is a person who knows who he or she is at all times by a feeling of connection to you center. When a master feels disconnected from their center, then he or she stands back and asks the self how he or she feels. He or she then identifies the feeling and makes a choice on it as to what is the best action to take.

- Identify what feels off about your life at the present moment
- Center yourself and become grounded
- Make a list of what is going on in your life
- Make a choice as to how you wish to proceed
- Give yourself comfort by asking the Spirit to take care of what you wish to accomplish in the best interest of the light

The Dai Koo Myo symbol vibrates through planes four, five and six

Dai	an adjective: big, magnificent, expansive
Koo	a picture of a man holding fire over his head, radiance, fire or light, expansion of light at the crown chakra
Myo	clairvoyance, green light piercing through the earthly planes to clear doubt, healing, piercing through the entire earthly world
Koo Myo	light of the Buddha's wisdom, expansive, all permeating light radiating (halo) from the head of the enlightened one

- Primarily used for attunements, empowerment and sealing things in people, places or things
- Creates the sun disk (energy focal point of source light)

Attunements

To receive your Dai Koo Myo symbol attunement please sit with your palms facing up on your lap and recite the following:

"Higher Self, I now accept the Dai Koo Myo symbol attunement prepared for me by Kiel Aman."

Attributes of the Dai Koo Myo symbol:

Color Visualize in Violet
Gemstone Place Phenacite or Petalite at the crown of your head

Sanskrit "Invincible Empowerment Mantra of Light"

Om amogha vairocana mahāmudrā maii padma jvāla pravarttaya hūm

A common practice for the Invincible Empowerment Mantra of Light was to sprinkle pure sand, blessed by this mantra, on the body of a deceased person or the person's tomb. The belief was that a person who had accumulated bad karma would be immediately freed and allowed a favorable rebirth.

Dai Koo Myo invocation

You are the magnificent expansive violet flame,
The all-seeing eye of the wisdom of the Buddha.
Descend from the fifth dimension and impart
Your radiant halo upon (name).

A Means to Awakening Spiritual Light

The mantra:

*"Om! Amogha Vairocana,
mahā-mudrā, mani-padma,
jvala pravartaya Hūm!"*

Meaning of the Dai Koo Myo Master Symbol

大	Da	Great
光	Guang	Ray of Light
明	Ming	Bright

Great Bright Light Ray: The spiritual light at the crown of the Buddha's head, a great canopy of white light

Invincible Empowerment Mantra of Light
The Invincible Empowerment Mantra of Light contains in its syllables the entire power of the omnipresent Mahâvairocana Buddha. When we recite the mantra earnestly, the Light of the Buddha will embrace us. Illusions will disappear as the moon becomes free from mist.

Translation of the Invincible Empowerment Mantra of Light:

"Om! Unfailing invincible universal light, great hand seal of authority, wish-fulfilling lotus gem of flaming light, please evolve forth, hum!"

Working with the Dai Koo Myo Master Symbol
In addition to the primary use of the Dai Koo Myo Master Symbol in the attunement process, this symbol is also used as a seal to lock in pre-programmed energies to act according to how they are instructed. This symbol is used as a seal to ensure that the process is fully actualized.

The Dai Koo Myo Master Symbol is also used in conjunction with the Hon Sha Zah Sho Nen Symbol, embodying the light of the sun and moon.

Harmony Treatment
(Body, Mind and Nervous System Treatment)

1. *Right hand on client's crown, left thunder fingers on client's third eye region*
2. *Right hand on client's crown, left thunder fingers on the tip of client's nose*
3. *Right hand on client's crown, left thunder fingers on the center of client's sternum*
4. *Right hand on client's crown, left thunder fingers on the base of client's solar plexus*
5. *Right hand on clients crown, left palm on the top edge of Client's pubis*
6. *Right hand under the center of client's sacrum, left hand on the top edge of client's pubis*
7. *Index and thumb of both hands at client's baby toe area*
8. *Cross-arm index fingers at client's inner ankle region*

What is a Connection?

- Opening a path that allows you to be with your spirit is connection.

- Struggle is a symptom of disconnection.

- Back off from struggle to maintain being connected.

- Ask spirit to make a connection with you.

- A master is a teacher and is always connected with spirit; a connected person is one who teaches by deeds and not just by mere words.

- When teaching and providing comfort to others, one should listen to what they are saying because they are teaching you as well.

- All of your clients are drawn to you as mirrors; therefore pay attention to what you are saying to them and what they are responding back to you; we are all connected in life through our issues.

- Follow your intuition as the mental body is not always in tune with the spiritual body.

- Fear is an opportunity to express power. Embrace and address your fears. (Stop - notice - ask for spirit for assistance)

- A hyperactive mental body (pre-occupied with stressful thoughts) draws one away from feeling connected.

- The role of an energy worker is to connect to the pulse of the universe and be in tune with the language of the soul.

- Discover your personal truth and be faithful to it always. As a rule of thumb, release all judgment and guilt.

Igniting the Body of Light

The Eighth (Spleen) Chakra

The eighth chakra is the center of your earthly grounding. This chakra represents the anchoring of the spirit to the physical body. It is the sole reason for our ability to be present in the midst of pain. The eighth chakra heals the physical body via the spleen, which also has the nature of containing the lifeblood of our existence by keeping the blood within veins, arteries and vessels.

This chakra is the center that holds the physical body together. It reflects our ability to satisfy our zest for life, accomplish our goals and survive being attacked. It allows us to transcend our fears and embrace our pains. This chakra is the chakra of physical life and the supporting rod of life. If this chakra fails to anchor or hold our lives through molecular cohesion, then we will ascend to another existence. The object of this center is to assist in grounding our spiritual essences in our physical forms in order to allow us to accomplish our life assignments prior to ascending to the next level of our evolution.

This chakra is to the left of the body just below the ribcage in the area of the spleen. In addition to having the attributes of the second Chakra, it is also the center that allows for the revitalization of the entire body environment. It is the doorway to the reception and assimilation of the life giving energies of the universe. The meridian or energy channel within the body it ties to is the spleen.

The eighth chakra combines with the root chakra to allow for the revitalization of the life force.

Short Self Treatment
Place your left palm on your spleen center and your right palm over the perineum to ignite the energy necessary to activate your life force.

The Ninth (Etheric Heart) Chakra
The ninth chakra (etheric heart) is the heart of the spirit. It is from this chakra that we receive the light of our spiritual essence, which means that the connection with the spirit resides in this center. It is within this center that the spirit interprets the growth of the body of man and the body of the soul. The thymus gland (is also known as the etheric heart) clears out poisons and toxins via the immune system. This center also allows us to purify the light of our ascended souls. It is the true house of ascension, the safe keeper of our spiritual essences. This center is our gateway to ascension through compassion for humanity.

The attributes of the ninth chakra are: ascension and faith, love and compassion, surrendering and trust, and honor and respect. The ninth chakra is also known as "The house of universal ascension." This chakra center is the doorway to the light of our heavenly spirit.

This chakra is located between the nipples and collarbone of the right pectoral muscle just outside of the sternum. It regulates the immune system via the thymus gland.

Short Self Treatment
Your palms must be used on the sites of the thymus and pineal glands, the left for the thymus and the right for the pineal. This will activate the gateway for illumination of the consciousness. Use the eighth chakra with the ninth chakra to allow for the energies of the heavens and the earth to permeate one's existence. Using the eighth chakra in conjunction with the ninth chakra strengthens the entire body and boosts one's immune system.

Short Self Treatment
Using the eighth and ninth chakras for healing assimilates the full spectrum of light, thus healing the entire body environment. Place the right hand on chakra eight and the left hand on chakra nine to seal the orbits connecting the spectrum body.

Trinity Treatment: *Uses the Dai Koo Myo symbol with the Hon Sha Zah Sho Nen symbol to invoke the body of light for programmed healing. This treatment is the coupling of the three methods mentioned above. Place your right palm on clients perineum center and your left palm on the clients eighth chakra (spleen center); recite the following invocation)*

"I choose to be that I am, I am (insert positive attribute you wish to bring about), upload"

Place your right palm on client's seventh chakra (crown) and your left palm on the clients ninth chakra (thymus center); recite the following invocation)

"I know that I am, I am (insert same positive attribute you wish to bring about), download"

Place your right palm on client's eighth chakra (spleen center) and your left palm on the client's ninth chakra (thymus center); recite the following invocation)

"All that is I am that I am, integrate"

*At each hand position, of the treatment routine above invoke the I am and insert the program (any negative patterns that you are trying to change stated in a positive manner). Then, invoke and draw the Dai Koo Myo and Hon Sha Zah Sho Nen symbols using your mind at each hand position. Finish by directing the energy flow, via saying (upload, download or integrate)

A Means to Awakening Spiritual Light

Embodiment of the Light of the Buddha's Meditation

Protruding Siddhi: Navel: **A Ra Pa Ca Na**: Christ Consciousness

Recite the Hon Sha Zah Sho Nen Invocation:
The universe is filled with power and mysteries.
I am the magnetic attraction of the light of life.
He who has the power of healing hands, power comes
Just as I summon the healing power.
I am given the power.
My hands behold the essence of the light of purity
And completely cures everyone they touch.
When my hands stretch forth,
They heal with light and love and power
"Hon Sha Zah Sho Nen."
You are the one who opens closed doors.
You are the one who closes open doors.
Open the doorway to the twelfth dimension.
Reconnect my 12 strands of DNA and open the way for the reception of the I Am Presence.
Close the doorway to all distortions hindering its reconnection and reception.

May the love of the one soul radiate upon you, (person's name), and permeate every part of your body, healing, soothing, strengthening and dissipating all that hinders service and good health.

A Means to Awakening Spiritual Light

- Visualize the *"Hon Sha Zah Sho Nen"* at your navel center.
- Visualize the *"Cosmic Stupa Hon Sha Zah Sho Nen"* at your navel center.
- Visualize the **A Ra Pa Ca Na** Siddham symbols 12 times at your navel center.

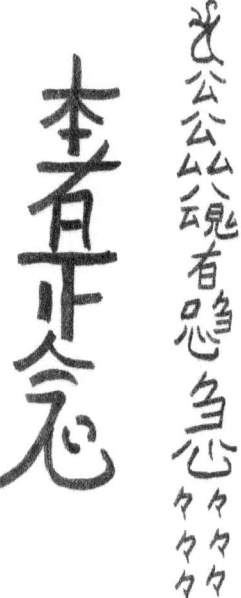

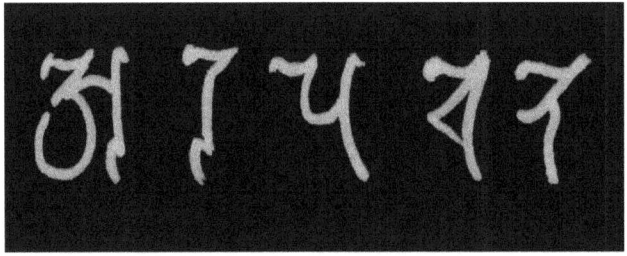

Intruding Siddhi: Heart: **A Vi Ra Hum Kham**: I Am Presence

Recite the Hon Sha Zah Sho Nen Invocation:
The universe is filled with power and mysteries.
I am the magnetic attraction of the light of life.
He who has the power of healing hands, power comes
Just as I summon the healing power.
I am given the power.
My hands behold the essence of the light of purity
And completely cures everyone they touch.
When my hands stretch forth,
They heal with light and love and power
"Hon Sha Zah Sho Nen."
You are the one who opens closed doors.
You are the one who closes open doors.
Open the doorway to the twelfth dimension.
Reconnect my 12 strands of DNA and open the way for the reception of the I Am Presence.
Close the doorway to all distortions hindering its reconnection and reception.

May the love of the one soul radiate upon you, (person's name), and permeate every part of your body, healing, soothing, strengthening and dissipating all that hinders service and good health.

A Means to Awakening Spiritual Light

- Visualize the *"Hon Sha Zah Sho Nen"* at your heart center.
- Visualize the *"Cosmic Stupa Hon Sha Zah Sho Nen"* at your heart center.
- Visualize the **A Vi Ra Hum Kham** Siddham symbols 12 times at your heart center.

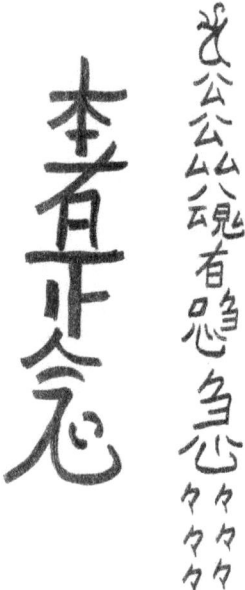

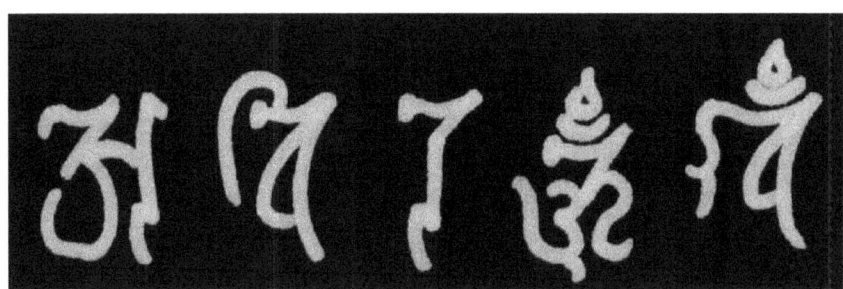

Upper Siddhi: 3rd Eye: **A Vam Ram Ham Kham**: Causal (Cosmic) Body

Recite the Hon Sha Zah Sho Nen Invocation:
The universe is filled with power and mysteries.
I am the magnetic attraction of the light of life.
He who has the power of healing hands, power comes
Just as I summon the healing power.
I am given the power.
My hands behold the essence of the light of purity
And completely cures everyone they touch.
When my hands stretch forth,
They heal with light and love and power
"Hon Sha Zah Sho Nen."
You are the one who opens closed doors.
You are the one who closes open doors.
Open the doorway to the twelfth dimension.
Reconnect my 12 strands of DNA and open the way for the reception of the I Am Presence.
Close the doorway to all distortions hindering its reconnection and reception.

May the love of the one soul radiate upon you, (person's name), and permeate every part of your body, healing, soothing, strengthening and dissipating all that hinders service and good health.

A Means to Awakening Spiritual Light

- Visualize the *"Hon Sha Zah Sho Nen"* at the 3rd eye center.
- Visualize the *"Cosmic Stupa Hon Sha Zah Sho Nen"* at the 3rd eye center.
- Visualize the **A Vam Ram Ham Kham** Siddham symbols 12 times at the third eye center.

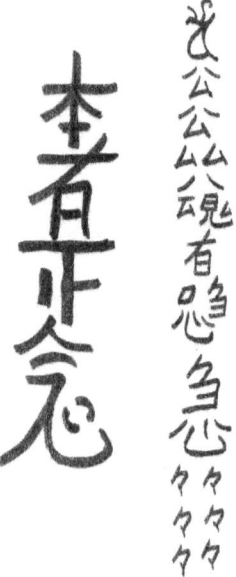

A Means to Awakening Spiritual Light

Recite the following invocation:

Dai Koo Myo,
You are the magnificent expansive violet flame, The all-seeing eye of the wisdom of the Buddha. Descend from the fifth dimension and impart Your radiant halo upon (name).

• Visualize the Dai Koo Myo symbol above the crown of your head.

Recite the Mantra of Light 21 times:

"*Om! Amogha vairocana, mahā-mudrā, mani-padma, jvala pravartaya hūm!*"

Prayer Formula
How to Elicit the Fullness of the Power of Prayer

Prayer in the truest sense of the word is the expression of the fullness of feeling that transmits through the emotions whether vocalized or not, but the vocalization of one's true feelings adds power to the intensity of the prayer. These emotions are transmitted to the universe through waves of sound, thus expressing an intense need to resolve any particular issue. The response from the universal is based upon the sound pattern sent, which allows for similar patterns to respond, thus mirroring your answer back to you and resolving the problem.

These patterns, however, are based on one's true feelings and not the feelings one projects to others. True prayer is based upon the expression of one's true intentions as generated by one's sincerity of one's feelings.

Invocational sound patterns are those frequencies that find harmony within one's own environment and will accumulate to either enhance a positive environment or further degrade a negative environment.

Evocational sound patterns are those frequencies that create discord in one's environment and will disperse in the form of protection in order to enhance a positive or negative expression, causing harm and disruption to the environment of another.

Prayer formula:

"**Focus** on your **Desire** with an **Intensity** of **Need** and then **Express** the **Intention** of the expected **Outcome**"

The universe is thought itself. This thought is the mind consciousness of what people term as God, Buddha, etc. All thought comes from the expressive universal od, Buddha, etc .

The Laws of U
(the Universal Mirror - Karma)

To Learn: To seek information about self-empowerment. One should always be watchful over one's purpose in life in order to allow for clarity of thought regarding one's aims and goals of one's personal desires.

To Grow: To become a better human being always be kind at heart and peaceful in one's demeanor in order to reap the benefits of one's growth.

To Express: To acknowledge what we learn, what we love and the reality of the spirit. Expression is our universal link to the reality of spiritual development through the expression of our experiences in life.

To Be:	Light:	Life needs to be free and joyful
	Brave:	Stand strong for what you believe
	Whole:	Accept the truth of who you are
To Feel:	Useful:	Be ready to assist those individuals in need
	Accepted:	Always allow for appreciation to be a part of your ability to be free to express what you are in truth and free to place yourself on the alter of self-evaluation

To Know: Truth, peace and balance. Truth allows you to free yourself from fear and the control of others. Peace comes from the satisfaction of being free to be who you really are, which allows your life to be balanced.

To Live: The cycle of love and light. Completion occurs when one comes to terms with the acceptance that your life is in the fullness of term (time of death in the worldly sense) and it is time to end the lesson to be reborn into the light of love.

Sensitivity and Pain

No one can cause anyone else emotional pain as this type of pain is and always will be a reflection of the truth that we are not willing to face about ourselves. Our true pain is a reflection of what we really want for ourselves and do not yet have. However, it is not only to accept who you really are, but also to embrace and love yourself unconditionally for what you think is good about yourself as well as what you think is bad about yourself. What you think is bad about yourself is often a truer reflection of what we are running away from; because this is the self we are usually hiding away from others finding out about and generally ashamed of. It, what we feel about ourselves, is always about us and the difficulties caused by others are always a reflection of what we are not willing to face about our own true natures.

"May the sacrifice of your pain be accepted.
May the acceptance of your pain grant you eternal life.
Let your prayers for balance be realized.
Let the one who is asking for salvation be granted inner peace."

Sensitivity: Defines the acceptance or expressions of how we feel or react when stimulated within our environments and determines the nature of our response.

Too much sensitivity makes one susceptible to emotional pain and being fragile in the mind. Being overly sensitive to others and the catering too much to the needs of others creates disempowerment and scatters the nervous system. This situation is known as raging fire.

Not enough sensitivity hardens the spirit, makes one callous in his expressions towards others in life, alienates one from the world and creates stagnation in the body. This situation is known as muddy water.

Expressions of Reflections

1
If one teaches one stupidity,
then one's stupidity will be stupid.

If one teaches one wisdom,
then one's wisdom will be wise.

If one teaches one foolishness,
then one's foolishness will be foolish.

It is better for one to tread the path in between the two (stupidity and foolishness), and walk with wisdom.

2

If one rushes through the patterns of life that one has come through without acknowledging the process or reflecting on the experience, then one would never be able to realize the changes that have occurred.

If one treads too carefully, while being totally absorbed within the process, then one will never be able to realize that there is hope and his life will be bitter.

However, if one boldly treads the path one step at a time and acknowledges the process, while continuously forging his way through life, then one will know where he comes from and where he is going.

3
"What am I doing to you?
I am feeding you the tail of the dragon so that your spirit may ascend."

"The soul of a dragon is found in its tail.
One should taste the dragon's tail, as the nature of the dragon is expressed in the tail whose nature is to swing freely.
To taste the soul of the dragon is to know what it is to be free.
If one is seeking to possess the tail of the dragon, then one is seeking to be set free.
It is important to taste the dragon's tail as it releases a captured soul and sets it free."

4
"Blessed are those who are meek at heart;
Blessed are those who release the fears of despair;
Blessed are those who accept the good things of life;
For these are of those whose hearts shall inherit the earth."
"You are now ready to accept the heart of your soul,

So we are ready to shower your being with the light of love.
You are now within the company of your ascended soul."

5
"The answer to all reason is always in the question.
Seek out why one asks the question and the answer is very close behind."

6
"Can there ever be peace without conflict?
Will there ever be conflict without resolution?
This is the nature of life and the reason why one is in the condition one is in at any given time."

7
"There is no way to predict the reason, but there is always an answer through the outcome."

8
"Consider the one thing that allows you to become the victor and then also consider the meaninglessness of worrying about the why. Rest assured, you are not going to lose, but for sure you are going to struggle. No matter what, whatever is will be."

9
When the mouth speaks, the heart feels.
When the heart feels, the will is accomplished.

10
As the eyes look beyond, they see the meaning of life.
Knowing that, with a single glance, eternal knowledge will be there forever within that single being.

That being will then know the pain, torture and confusion of life for humans living within the unexplored, wide universe; each universe being confined inside another.

11
Yesterday's deeds are today's memories.
Do not allow today's memories to become tomorrow's despair.

12
Who am I?
I am opening my vest so that you may see me.
I am he who God hears.
I am he who God understands.
I am he who understands God.
I am he who is obedient to God.
I am the mouth that speaks.
I am the heart that feels.
I am the will that accomplishes.
I am the two halves of an incomplete whole.
1 am your worst enemy.
I am your best friend.
I am he whose existence alone challenges
what you say you believe.
I am the one who makes you accountable
for what you say.
I am your deepest pain. I am your truest love.
My presence alone stirs up your true inner being.
My touch penetrates your blockages and removes distrust.
My words shatter all of your defensive barriers.
I am the hidden reflections of your deepest truth.
I am the light that dispels your deepest darkness.
I am the savior who rescues you from
the harm you do to yourself.
I am your reflection.

A Means Awakening Spiritual Light

97

A Means to Awakening Spiritual Light

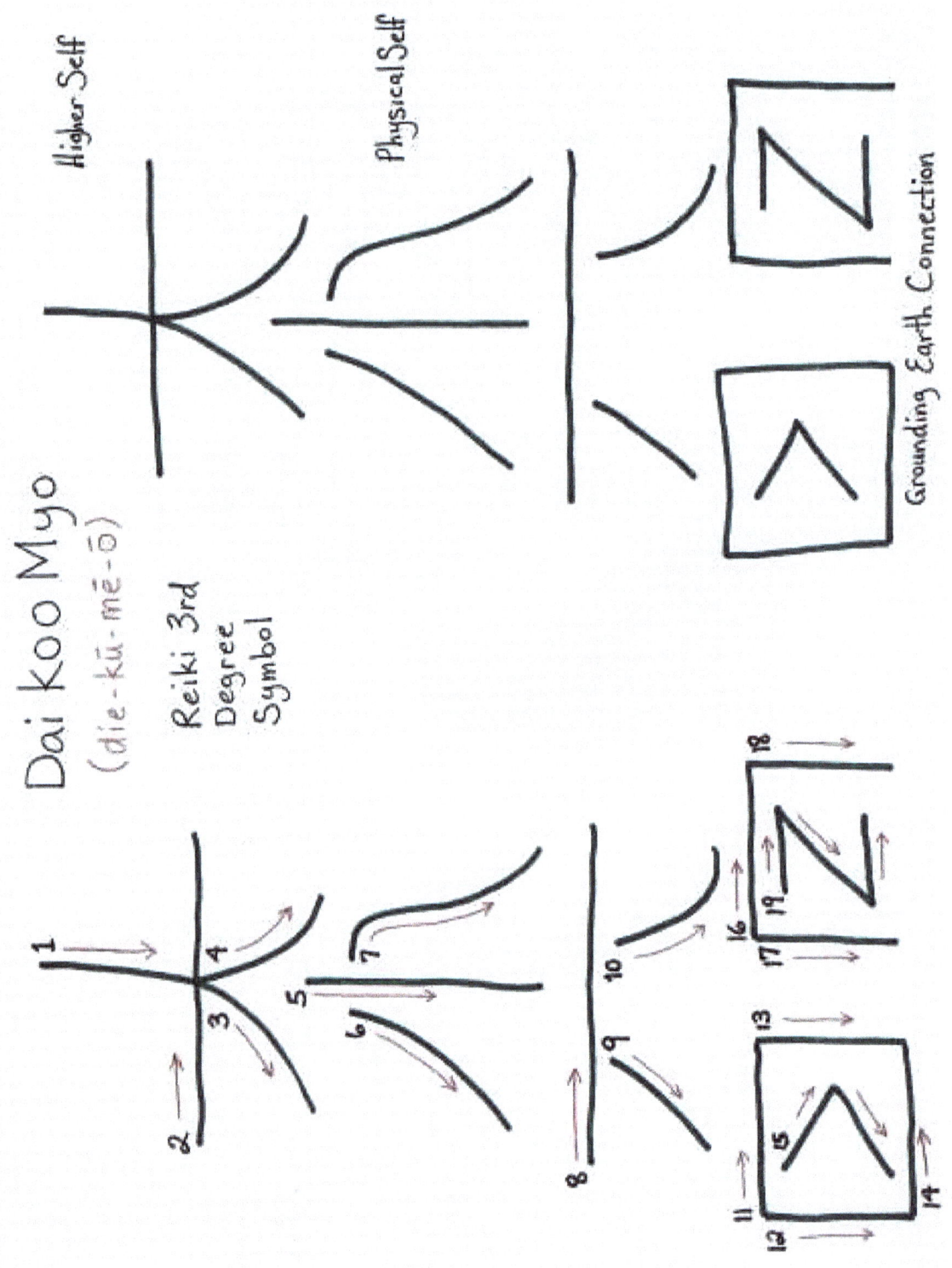

A Means Awakening Spiritual Light

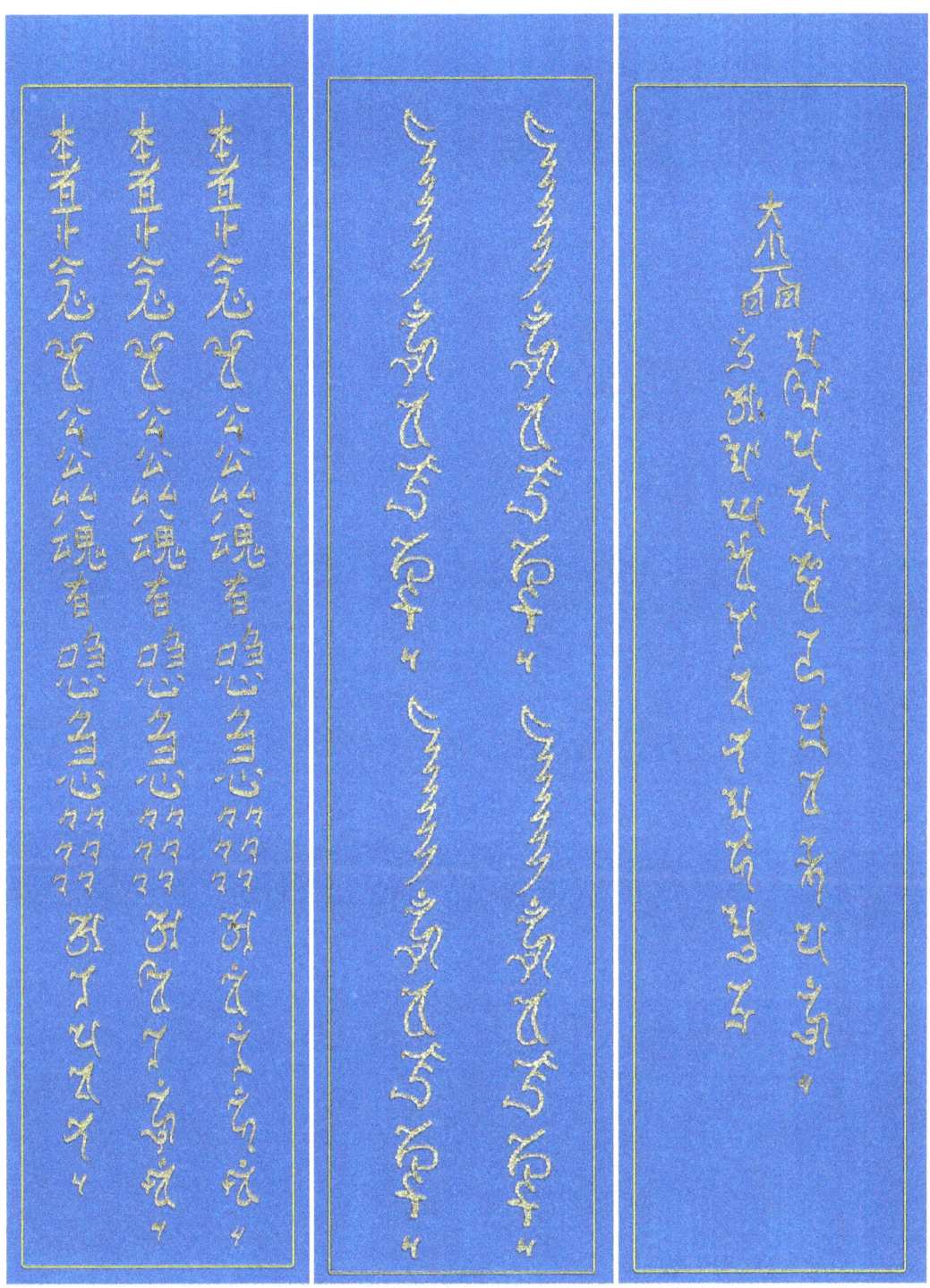

A Means to Awakening Spiritual Light

www.ingramcontent.com/pod-product-compliance
Lightning Source LLC
Chambersburg PA
CBHW061119010526
44112CB00024B/2915